Disclaimer:

The information in this travel guide is intended for general reference only. While efforts have been made to ensure accuracy at the time of publication, the author and publisher do not guarantee the information's completeness or reliability. Travel conditions and details can change, and it is the reader's responsibility to verify critical information such as transportation, accommodations, and safety guidelines directly with relevant sources.

The author and publisher are not liable for any loss, injury, or inconvenience resulting from the use of this guide. Recommendations are based on personal opinions and experiences and do not constitute endorsements. Readers are advised to exercise caution, use discretion, and consider their own safety and health when traveling.

TABLE OF CONTENTS

Chapter 4: Accommodations and Practical Travel Information

Accommodation Options

- ★ Luxury Hotels, Boutique Stays, Budget Options, and Farm Stays
- ★ Recommended Hotels with Contact Information

Travel Essentials

- ★ Banks, ATMs, and Financial Services
- ★ Local Laws, Customs, and Language Tips
- ★ Health, Safety, and Travel Insurance

Chapter 5: Transportation and Getting Around Burgundy

Transportation

- ★ Getting to Burgundy: Airlines, Trains, and Buses
- ★ Car Rentals, Bicycle Rentals, and Local Transportation Options
- ★ Driving Tips and Directions to Tourist Centers
- ★ Maps and Navigation

Chapter 6: Burgundy's Culture and Traditions

Customs and Traditions

- ★ Festivals and Events in 2025
- ★ Social Etiquette, Religious Practices, and Cultural Behavior

CHAPTER ONE

Introduction to Burgundy

Overview of Burgundy

Burgundy, or Bourgogne in French, is a historical region in central-eastern France, known for its rich cultural heritage, world-class wines, and picturesque landscapes. It boasts a harmonious blend of medieval architecture, rolling vineyards, and charming towns. Stretching from Dijon to the north and Mâcon to the south, Burgundy has long been a haven for travelers seeking a mix of history, gastronomy, and outdoor adventure.

Famed for its vineyards, Burgundy is one of the most prestigious wine-producing regions in the world, with wines such as Pinot Noir and Chardonnay gaining international acclaim. The Côte d'Or, a wine-growing area, is a must-visit for wine lovers. Beyond wine, the region is also renowned for its cuisine, offering dishes like boeuf bourguignon, coq au vin, and escargot, showcasing local flavors.

Burgundy's history dates back centuries, with Romanesque abbeys, medieval castles, and Gothic cathedrals scattered across the region. The capital, Dijon, was once home to the Dukes of Burgundy and is filled with historical landmarks, including the Palace of the Dukes and Notre-Dame de Dijon. Beaune, another notable town, is famous for the Hospices de Beaune, an architectural marvel and symbol of the region's charitable history.

For nature lovers, Burgundy offers pristine landscapes, from the Morvan Regional Natural Park to serene rivers like the Yonne and Saône, perfect for hiking, cycling, and outdoor exploration.

Whether you're exploring charming villages, sampling fine wine, or wandering through its storied past, Burgundy offers an unforgettable experience for every type of traveler.

Why Visit Burgundy in 2025?

Visiting Burgundy in 2025 offers a rare opportunity to experience this iconic region at the height of its cultural, culinary, and natural splendor. 2025 marks an exciting year filled with special events, new developments in tourism, and enhanced experiences for travelers. From historic vineyard tours to immersive local festivals, Burgundy will be a top destination for both seasoned travelers and first-time visitors.

As the world emerges from global changes, Burgundy is positioning itself as a sustainable and eco-friendly travel destination, with increasing attention on preserving its landscapes and traditions. Tourists can expect more eco-tourism options, green accommodations, and guided tours that emphasize the preservation of Burgundy's cultural and natural treasures. The blend of modern comfort and historical significance makes 2025 an exceptional time to explore.

Additionally, Burgundy is known for its vibrant calendar of events, and 2025 will feature exciting festivals, wine harvest celebrations, and cultural exhibits that showcase the region's rich heritage. This year will also introduce enhanced travel routes and upgraded visitor services, making Burgundy more accessible than ever before.

Burgundy's Unique Appeal: History, Culture, and Adventure

Burgundy offers a diverse mix of attractions that appeal to lovers of history, culture, and adventure alike. Its unique charm lies in the combination of world-class wine, centuries-old traditions, and opportunities for thrilling outdoor activities.

History

Burgundy is a region steeped in history, with roots stretching back thousands of years. From ancient Roman settlements to a powerful medieval duchy, Burgundy has played a central role in European history, influencing art, politics, religion, and, of course, viticulture.

1. Ancient Beginnings and Roman Influence

The history of Burgundy begins long before the Romans, with the region originally inhabited by Celtic tribes. By the 1st century BC, the Romans arrived and established Augustodunum (modern-day Autun) as a prominent city in their province of Gallia Lugdunensis. The Romans brought with them viticulture, laying the foundation for what would become Burgundy's world-famous wine industry. Numerous Roman roads and ruins, such as the Temple of Janus and the Theatre of Autun, can still be found in the region, highlighting its historical importance during this period.

2. The Rise of the Kingdom of Burgundy

After the fall of the Western Roman Empire, the Burgundians, a Germanic tribe, migrated to the area in the 5th century AD. They established the Kingdom of Burgundy, which became part of the larger Frankish Empire after being conquered by the Merovingian kings in the late 6th century. The kingdom's territory shifted and evolved over time, eventually becoming part of the Carolingian Empire under Charlemagne.

3. The Birth of the Duchy of Burgundy (9th Century)

In the 9th century, the Duchy of Burgundy was established as a powerful feudal state within the Kingdom of France. The dukes of Burgundy, particularly from the 14th to the 15th centuries, were among the most powerful and influential rulers in Europe. The duchy stretched across much of modern-day eastern France and even parts of the Low Countries (present-day Belgium and the Netherlands), becoming a major political and cultural force.

4. The Golden Age of the Duchy (14th–15th Century)

The House of Valois-Burgundy led Burgundy through its golden age, with dukes such as Philip the Bold (1363–1404), John the Fearless (1404–1419), Philip the Good (1419–1467), and Charles the Bold (1467–1477) leaving a significant legacy. These rulers not only strengthened the duchy through diplomacy and warfare but also fostered a period of great cultural flourishing. The Burgundian court became a center for the arts, attracting poets, musicians, and artists from across Europe. The Burgundian School of Music and the rich artistic tradition of the region played a critical role in the development of the Northern Renaissance.

Burgundy's wealth largely came from its strategic position and the prosperity of its vineyards, wool, and textile industries. The dukes maintained a delicate balance of power with both the French monarchy and the Holy Roman Empire, often acting as intermediaries in European politics.

5. The Fall of Burgundy and Annexation to France (1477)

The death of Charles the Bold in 1477 marked the end of Burgundy's political independence. Charles died in the Battle of Nancy during a failed campaign, and his only heir, Mary of Burgundy, could not maintain control of the duchy. Burgundy was subsequently annexed by France under King Louis XI. Although the duchy ceased to exist as an independent state, its cultural and historical legacy continued to shape the region.

6. The Renaissance and Religious Turmoil (16th–17th Century)

During the Renaissance, Burgundy remained a prosperous part of France, thanks largely to its agricultural and wine production. However, the region was also affected by the French Wars of Religion in the late 16th century, as tensions between Catholics and Protestants (Huguenots) erupted into violence. Several towns in Burgundy became centers of conflict during these wars, which eventually led to the rise of Henry IV and the Edict of Nantes in 1598, ensuring religious tolerance for Protestants.

7. The Modern Era: Burgundy in Revolutionary and Napoleonic France

The French Revolution in 1789 radically altered Burgundy's political landscape. The feudal system that had long defined the region was dismantled, and Burgundy, like the rest of France, was reorganized into departments. The revolutionaries abolished the privileges of the nobility, and many historic estates were confiscated or sold off. The region's rural population, heavily reliant on agriculture and wine production, adapted to these dramatic changes.

Under Napoleon Bonaparte, Burgundy played a role in France's territorial expansion, and the Code Napoléon reorganized the legal framework, giving the region stability. During this period, Burgundy's vineyards continued to gain prestige, with the Burgundy wine classification system formalized in the 19th century.

8. Burgundy in the 20th Century

The 20th century brought both challenges and progress to Burgundy. World Wars I and II had a significant impact on the region, with many towns and villages affected by the fighting. The French Resistance was active in Burgundy during World War II, and several key battles and operations took place in the region.

After the war, Burgundy experienced modernization and economic growth, largely driven by its agricultural and wine industries. The development of wine tourism in the second half of the 20th century brought international attention to Burgundy's vineyards. The region's wine industry was further cemented as one of the finest in the world, with appellations like Romanée-Conti becoming symbols of luxury and refinement.

9. Burgundy Today: A Blend of Tradition and Modernity

Today, Burgundy remains a symbol of elegance, history, and cultural heritage. It continues to be a leader in the production of world-class wines, with its vineyards recognized as a UNESCO World Heritage Site in 2015. The region's historic cities, like Dijon, Beaune, and Autun, along with its picturesque countryside, attract tourists from around the world.

Burgundy also preserves its rich architectural heritage, with Romanesque churches, medieval abbeys like Cluny and Fontenay, and châteaux scattered throughout the landscape. The region's culinary and wine traditions remain central to its identity, making Burgundy a destination where the past and present coexist harmoniously.

Culture

Burgundy's culture is a rich tapestry woven from centuries of history, deeply rooted traditions, and an enduring appreciation for the finer things in life—particularly its world-famous wine and culinary arts. The region's unique blend of French and

Burgundian identity is reflected in its architecture, festivals, local customs, and the arts, creating a vibrant and inviting atmosphere for visitors.

1. The Wine Culture: Burgundy's Heart and Soul

Wine is more than just a product in Burgundy—it is an integral part of the region's identity and culture. The history of winemaking in Burgundy dates back over 2,000 years to the Roman era, and since then, it has become synonymous with some of the most prestigious wines in the world. Burgundy's vineyards, known as climats, are a UNESCO World Heritage Site, and they symbolize the intimate relationship between the land, the people, and their centuries-old winemaking traditions.

Wine is a way of life in Burgundy, influencing not only the economy but also the cultural and social practices. Many villages and towns are centered around their vineyards, and locals take pride in their deep knowledge of viticulture. Festivals like the Saint-Vincent Tournante celebrate the patron saint of winemakers and bring communities together for a weekend of wine tasting, parades, and festivities.

Visitors to Burgundy will find that wine is central to many aspects of local culture, from food pairings in restaurants to organized wine tours and tasting sessions. Wine is not just a drink, but an art form, and understanding the region's terroir, appellations, and history is considered a vital part of experiencing Burgundy's culture.

2. Culinary Traditions

Burgundy's culinary scene is famous worldwide, and the region has made significant contributions to French gastronomy. The cuisine reflects the region's agricultural bounty and an emphasis on rich, hearty flavors. Burgundy is the birthplace of several iconic dishes that are now staples of French cuisine:

- **Bœuf Bourguignon:** A slow-cooked beef stew made with red Burgundy wine, onions, carrots, mushrooms, and herbs.
- **Coq au Vin:** A dish of chicken braised in wine, typically made with red Burgundy wine, bacon, mushrooms, and garlic.

- **Escargots de Bourgogne**: Snails cooked in garlic butter, parsley, and wine, a delicacy often associated with Burgundy.
- **Œufs en Meurette**: Poached eggs served in a rich red wine sauce with bacon and mushrooms.
- **Epoisses Cheese**: A soft and pungent cheese, Epoisses is one of Burgundy's finest culinary exports, known for its strong flavor and washed rind.

Dijon, the capital of Burgundy, is particularly famous for its mustard, and moutarde de Dijon is a key ingredient in many Burgundian recipes. Burgundy is also home to a wide array of artisan products, including honey, truffles, and charcuterie, often featured at local markets.

The region's farm-to-table ethos and emphasis on seasonal, local ingredients highlight the importance of sustainability and tradition in Burgundian cuisine.

3. Festivals and Celebrations

Burgundy is home to a variety of festivals throughout the year that celebrate the region's history, wine, and culture. These events bring both locals and visitors together to enjoy music, food, and festivities.

- **Saint-Vincent Tournante:** This annual festival takes place in a different wine-producing village each year. It honors Saint Vincent, the patron saint of winemakers, and includes processions, wine tastings, and a ceremonial blessing of the wine.
- **Hospices de Beaune Wine Auction**: Held in November, this is one of the most famous wine auctions in the world. The auction is part of a weekend-long celebration of Burgundy's wine culture, with tastings, markets, and charity events.
- **Dijon International Gastronomy Fair**: One of the largest food and wine events in France, this fair showcases the best of Burgundy's culinary traditions alongside international foods and wines.

- **Fête de la Musique**: Like the rest of France, Burgundy participates in the Fête de la Musique in June, with live music performances in towns and villages, celebrating local musicians and artists.
- **Cluny Horse Festival**: Celebrating the region's equestrian heritage, this festival showcases horse riding, racing, and performances in the historic town of Cluny.

These festivals not only highlight Burgundy's cultural heritage but also foster a sense of community among locals and offer visitors an immersive experience.

4. Religious and Architectural Heritage

Burgundy has a strong religious and architectural heritage, particularly evident in its Romanesque churches, abbeys, and monasteries. The region was a significant center of Christianity during the Middle Ages, and its abbeys played a crucial role in shaping religious life in Europe.

- **Abbey of Cluny**: Founded in 910, Cluny was one of the largest and most influential monasteries in medieval Europe. Although much of the original structure was destroyed during the French Revolution, the remains of the abbey still attract visitors who want to learn about its historical importance.

- **Fontenay Abbey**: A UNESCO World Heritage Site, this Cistercian abbey is one of the best-preserved examples of medieval monastic architecture in Europe. It showcases the simplicity and austerity of Cistercian design, in contrast to the grandeur of Cluny.
- **Vézelay Basilica**: The Basilica of Sainte-Marie-Madeleine in Vézelay is another UNESCO World Heritage Site. This Romanesque masterpiece is a major pilgrimage site and was an important starting point for pilgrims heading to Santiago de Compostela.

Throughout Burgundy, visitors can explore a wealth of medieval churches, châteaux, and fortresses, reflecting the region's long and storied past.

5. Language and Dialects

While French is the official language of Burgundy, the region has its own historical dialects, such as Burgundian (Bourguignon), which is a variation of the Oïl language family that includes French. Although Burgundian dialect is no longer widely spoken, it remains a part of the region's cultural heritage, and some older generations still use certain expressions or words from the local dialect.

Today, French is spoken with a distinctive Burgundian accent in rural areas, and the region is known for its politeness and formality, particularly in small towns where local customs are still strong.

6. Arts and Crafts

Burgundy has a rich tradition of artisan craftsmanship, which includes pottery, ceramics, and tapestries. The town of Nevers is known for its faïence pottery, a type of tin-glazed earthenware that has been produced in the region since the 16th century.

Beaune and Dijon are also centers for the arts, with several galleries showcasing both traditional and contemporary works by local artists. The Burgundian School of Music from the medieval period contributed to the development of polyphonic music, and this musical heritage is still celebrated in concerts and festivals across the region.

Tapestry making was historically important in Burgundy, with notable workshops producing elaborate tapestries for the dukes and religious institutions. Some of these ancient traditions continue to thrive in local artisan workshops, where visitors can purchase hand-crafted items that reflect Burgundy's artistic heritage.

7. Traditions and Customs

Burgundy's traditions are closely tied to its agricultural and wine-producing roots. The pace of life in the region reflects a respect for the land, with an emphasis on slow living and enjoying simple pleasures like food, wine, and community gatherings.

- **Wine Harvest Festivals**: Each autumn, the grape harvest is a time of celebration in Burgundy. Workers and locals come together to celebrate the end of the harvest season, often with communal meals, music, and wine.
- **Seasonal Markets**: Traditional markets in towns and villages remain a vital part of local life. These markets offer fresh produce, cheeses, meats, and artisan goods, and they are also social events where neighbors catch up and visitors can experience the local flavor.

Burgundy is a region that takes pride in its traditions and the preservation of its cultural heritage, making it a destination where visitors can truly experience authentic French life.

Adventure

Burgundy is more than just wine and history—it's a paradise for adventure seekers who crave outdoor activities, unique experiences, and thrilling explorations in the heart of nature. From hiking and cycling through vineyards and rolling hills to canoeing on tranquil rivers, Burgundy offers a wealth of opportunities for active travelers. The region's varied landscapes, from peaceful waterways to rugged cliffs, provide the perfect backdrop for adventure-filled vacations.

1. Hiking Trails and Nature Walks

Burgundy boasts a vast network of hiking trails that wind through its picturesque countryside, vineyards, forests, and natural parks. Whether you're a casual walker or an avid hiker, there are trails to suit all levels of experience.

- **The Burgundy Wine Trail (Route des Grands Crus)**: This iconic trail takes hikers through some of the world's most famous vineyards. Along the way, you'll pass charming villages like Beaune, Nuits-Saint-Georges, and Gevrey-Chambertin, offering not just breathtaking views but also the chance to stop at wine estates for tastings.
- **Morvan Regional Natural Park:** Known as the "green heart" of Burgundy, Morvan is a vast natural park that offers stunning landscapes of forests, lakes, and mountains. There are numerous marked trails, such as the GR13 and GR de Pays Tour du Morvan, where hikers can explore hidden waterfalls, panoramic vistas, and peaceful woodland.
- **Vézelay to Santiago de Compostela**: For those seeking a spiritual adventure, the pilgrimage route from Vézelay to Santiago de Compostela in

Spain passes through Burgundy. The first leg of this famous trail is a rewarding walk through rolling hills, ancient towns, and historic churches.

2. Cycling and Mountain Biking

Burgundy is one of the best regions in France for cycling, with its quiet country roads, dedicated bike paths, and scenic routes through vineyards, villages, and along canals. Whether you're cycling for leisure or looking for more challenging rides, Burgundy offers a variety of experiences.

- **La Voie des Vignes**: This 22-kilometer cycling route takes you through the heart of Burgundy's wine country, connecting Beaune to Santenay. You'll ride past the famous vineyards of Pommard, Meursault, and Puligny-Montrachet, with plenty of opportunities to stop for wine tastings.

- **The Burgundy Canal (Canal de Bourgogne):** For a more leisurely ride, the towpath along the Burgundy Canal is ideal. The Canal Greenway stretches for 200 kilometers and passes through beautiful countryside, charming villages, and historic locks. It's perfect for families or those looking for a relaxing cycling adventure.
- **Mountain Biking in Morvan**: The Morvan Massif offers rugged terrain for more adventurous mountain bikers. With dense forests, steep hills, and challenging trails, Morvan provides a thrilling ride for those seeking a more demanding outdoor experience.

3. Water Sports and River Adventures
Burgundy's rivers and lakes offer an exciting range of water-based activities, from canoeing and kayaking to fishing and stand-up paddleboarding. The peaceful waterways allow adventurers to explore Burgundy from a different perspective, winding through valleys, under medieval bridges, and past quaint villages.

- **Canoeing and Kayaking on the Cure and Yonne Rivers**: The rivers Cure and Yonne provide some of the best spots for canoeing and kayaking in Burgundy. The Cure River, in particular, flows through the Morvan Regional Natural Park, offering stretches of calm water perfect for beginners, as well as more adventurous rapids for experienced paddlers.

- **Sailing and Water Sports on Lac des Settons**: One of the largest lakes in Burgundy, Lac des Settons in Morvan is a hub for water activities. Visitors can rent sailboats, kayaks, or paddleboards, and enjoy the lake's serene beauty. There are also opportunities for fishing and swimming.

- **Rafting and Canyoning:** For thrill-seekers, the Morvan region offers opportunities for rafting and canyoning in its more fast-flowing rivers. These activities are best suited for adventurous travelers looking to add some excitement to their trip.

4. Hot Air Ballooning

One of the most breathtaking ways to experience Burgundy's beauty is from the sky. Hot air ballooning over the vineyards and rolling hills of Burgundy offers an unforgettable adventure. Balloon rides typically launch from areas around Beaune or Dijon, taking passengers on a serene flight over châteaux, vineyards, and scenic landscapes.

This peaceful yet exhilarating experience allows travelers to appreciate Burgundy's stunning natural beauty in a unique way, and it's particularly enchanting at sunrise or sunset when the region is bathed in golden light.

5. Rock Climbing and Caving

For those who love the thrill of rock climbing, Burgundy has several excellent climbing spots, ranging from beginner-friendly areas to more challenging cliffs for experienced climbers.

- **Hauteroche Cliffs**: Located near Semur-en-Auxois, these limestone cliffs offer a variety of climbing routes for different skill levels. The panoramic views from the top make the climb even more rewarding.
- **Saffres**: This site, near Vitteaux, is another popular destination for climbers. The limestone walls provide routes of varying difficulty, making it a favorite for both beginners and seasoned climbers.
- **Caving in Morvan:** The Morvan Massif is also home to fascinating cave systems that are open to exploration. The Grotte de Champ Retard and Grotte de Saint-Romain offer guided caving experiences for adventurers looking to discover the underground world of Burgundy.

6. Horseback Riding

Horseback riding is a popular way to explore the scenic landscapes of Burgundy. Riding through vineyards, forests, and along rivers offers a peaceful and immersive adventure.

- **Equestrian Trails in Morvan:** The Morvan Regional Natural Park offers several horseback riding trails, allowing riders to experience the park's natural beauty at a leisurely pace. Riders can choose from short excursions or multi-day treks through the forested hills and open meadows.
- **Vineyard Horseback Tours**: In the heart of Burgundy's wine country, horseback tours are available that take riders through some of the most beautiful vineyard landscapes, providing a unique perspective on the region's agricultural heritage.

7. Airborne Adventures: Paragliding and Microlighting

For thrill-seekers who want to experience the adrenaline rush of flying, Burgundy offers several airborne adventures, including paragliding and microlighting. These activities provide a bird's-eye view of Burgundy's stunning terrain, from its vineyards and fields to its forests and lakes.

- **Paragliding in Morvan**: The Morvan area offers ideal conditions for paragliding, with its hills and valleys providing the perfect launch points for soaring through the air. Beginners can join tandem flights with experienced pilots, while seasoned adventurers can enjoy solo flights over the beautiful landscapes.
- **Microlight Flights**: For those looking for a motorized flight experience, microlight flights are available in several areas of Burgundy, including near Dijon and Beaune. These small aircraft offer a thrilling yet safe way to take in panoramic views of the region from above.

8. Wildlife Watching and Eco-Tourism

Burgundy's diverse ecosystems make it an excellent destination for wildlife enthusiasts. Morvan Regional Natural Park is a haven for nature lovers, with opportunities for birdwatching, wildlife tracking, and eco-tourism.

- **Birdwatching**: The park's wetlands and forests are home to a variety of bird species, including hawks, owls, and migratory birds. Several birdwatching hides are located throughout the park, offering excellent viewing points.

- **Nature Safaris**: Guided wildlife safaris in Morvan provide opportunities to spot deer, wild boar, and other native species in their natural habitats. These tours are perfect for families or individuals looking to connect with nature in an educational and exciting way.

CHAPTER TWO

Exploring Burgundy's Attractions

Top Tourist Attractions

Must-See Landmarks in Burgundy

Burgundy is home to some of the most iconic and historically significant landmarks in France. Each site tells a story of the region's rich history, religious heritage, and cultural importance. Here are the must-see landmarks that no visitor to Burgundy should miss:

1. Hospices de Beaune

- **Location:** Beaune
- **Overview:** Known for its stunning Gothic architecture and colorful glazed-tile roof, the Hospices de Beaune, or Hôtel-Dieu, was founded in 1443 as a hospital for the poor. Today, it stands

as one of the most beautiful buildings in France and is home to an annual wine auction that draws international visitors. Inside, visitors can explore the museum and its impressive collection of medieval art, including The Last Judgement by Rogier van der Weyden.

2. Abbaye de Fontenay

- **Location**: Montbard
- **Overview**: A UNESCO World Heritage site, this Cistercian abbey, founded in 1118, is one of the best-preserved medieval monasteries in Europe. The abbey's architecture exemplifies the simplicity and spirituality of Cistercian design, with its Romanesque buildings surrounded by peaceful gardens and woodland. Highlights include the church, cloisters, and the medieval forge.

3. Palace of the Dukes and States of Burgundy

- **Location:** Dijon
- **Overview**: This grand palace was once the seat of power for the Dukes of Burgundy, who ruled one of the most powerful territories in Europe during the Middle Ages. Today, the palace houses the Musée des Beaux-Arts de Dijon, featuring art collections that span centuries, from ancient Egypt to modern masterpieces. Visitors can also explore the Tour Philippe le Bon, a 46-meter tower offering panoramic views of Dijon.

4. Basilica of Sainte-Marie-Madeleine (Vézelay)

- **Location**: Vézelay
- **Overview**: Another UNESCO World Heritage site, this Romanesque basilica is located on a hill in the medieval town of Vézelay and is a key stop on the pilgrimage route to Santiago de Compostela. The basilica is renowned for its stunning sculpture work and peaceful atmosphere, attracting both pilgrims and art lovers. From the basilica, visitors can enjoy breathtaking views of the surrounding countryside.

5. Cluny Abbey

- **Location**: Cluny
- **Overview**: Founded in 910, Cluny Abbey was one of the most powerful and influential monasteries in medieval Europe. Though much of the abbey was destroyed during the French Revolution, the remaining structures still offer a glimpse into its grandeur. Visitors can explore the ruins, the surviving abbey church, and the impressive Farinier (granary). Cluny also serves as a historical hub for Romanesque architecture in Burgundy.

6. Château de La Rochepot

- **Location:** La Rochepot
- **Overview**: This striking medieval castle, perched on a hilltop surrounded by forests and vineyards, offers a picture-perfect view of Burgundy's feudal past. With its steep, tiled roof and fortified towers, Château de La Rochepot is a symbol of Burgundy's medieval history. Visitors can explore the castle's interiors, including the armory, living quarters, and chapel, while learning about its storied past.

7. Musée des Beaux-Arts de Dijon
- **Location**: Dijon
- **Overview**: Located in the Palace of the Dukes, this museum is one of the oldest and most renowned in France. It houses a vast collection of fine art, ranging from ancient antiquities to contemporary works. Highlights include the Tombs of the Dukes of Burgundy, which are intricate masterpieces of Gothic art, and a remarkable collection of paintings, sculptures, and decorative arts from various periods.

8. Château de Bussy-Rabutin
- **Location**: Bussy-le-Grand
- **Overview**: This Renaissance château is set in the heart of the Auxois countryside. It was the home of Roger de Bussy-Rabutin, a courtier and writer who fell out of favor with Louis XIV. The château is famous for its richly decorated interiors, especially its Hall of Portraits, which features satirical portraits painted by Bussy-Rabutin during his exile. The château's surrounding gardens are a peaceful place for a leisurely stroll.

9. Grottes d'Arcy-sur-Cure

- **Location**: Arcy-sur-Cure
- **Overview**: These prehistoric caves, located near Auxerre, contain some of the oldest cave paintings in Europe, dating back more than 28,000 years. Visitors can tour the network of caves to see the ancient art, which includes images of animals, human figures, and mysterious symbols. The caves also feature impressive stalactites and stalagmites formed over millennia.

10. Château de Cormatin

- **Location**: Cormatin
- **Overview**: Situated between Cluny and Tournus, this beautiful Renaissance château is known for its lavishly decorated interiors, which have been remarkably well-preserved. The grand spiral staircase, painted ceilings, and 17th-century rooms offer visitors a glimpse into the opulence of the period. The château is surrounded by a vast park with stunning French formal gardens, including a maze and water features.

Beautiful Villages and Towns in Burgundy

Burgundy is home to some of France's most picturesque villages and charming towns, each offering a unique blend of history, architecture, and local culture. Exploring these destinations allows visitors to experience the region's authentic charm, from bustling markets to peaceful countryside views. Here are some of the most beautiful villages and towns in Burgundy that should be on every traveler's itinerary:

1. Dijon

- **Overview**: The capital of Burgundy and a vibrant cultural hub, Dijon is renowned for its medieval and Renaissance architecture, rich history, and culinary delights. Its historic center is a UNESCO World Heritage site, filled with well-preserved buildings, including the Palace of the Dukes of Burgundy and the Church of Notre-Dame. Dijon is also the birthplace of mustard, and visitors can explore local markets, charming squares, and wine cellars.

- **Must-See**: Palace of the Dukes, Musée des Beaux-Arts, the Owl Trail (self-guided walking tour).

2. Beaune

- **Overview**: Beaune is the wine capital of Burgundy, famous for its role in the production and trading of Burgundy wines. The town's medieval center is beautifully preserved, with cobbled streets, half-timbered houses, and impressive Gothic buildings. Beaune is home to the famous Hospices de Beaune, a stunning historical hospital that now houses a museum. The town also hosts an annual wine auction that draws enthusiasts from all over the world.
- **Must-See**: Hospices de Beaune, the Collegiate Church of Notre-Dame, wine cellars and tasting tours.

3. Chablis

- **Overview**: Nestled in the northern part of Burgundy, Chablis is synonymous with world-class white wine. This small village is surrounded by vineyards, offering a tranquil and scenic escape for wine lovers. Chablis has a long wine-making tradition, and visitors can explore local wineries, taste the famous Chardonnay, and enjoy walking through the picturesque vineyard landscapes.
- **Must-See**: Wine tours and tastings at local domaines, the Saint-Martin Church.

4. Autun

- **Overview**: A town with a rich Roman heritage, Autun boasts impressive ancient ruins alongside beautiful medieval architecture. Founded by the Romans as Augustodunum, Autun is home to significant historical sites, including a Roman amphitheater, ancient gates, and a temple. The town's magnificent Cathedral of Saint-Lazare is a masterpiece of Romanesque art, famous for its intricately sculpted tympanum.
- **Must-See**: Roman amphitheater, Temple of Janus, Cathedral of Saint-Lazare.

5. Vézelay

- **Overview:** Perched on a hilltop, Vézelay is a UNESCO World Heritage site and one of the most picturesque medieval villages in Burgundy. The town's centerpiece is the Basilica of Sainte-Marie-Madeleine, a major pilgrimage site along the route to Santiago de Compostela. The village's narrow streets, lined with old stone houses, lead visitors to stunning views of the surrounding Morvan countryside.
- **Must-See**: Basilica of Sainte-Marie-Madeleine, panoramic views, art galleries and local craft shops.

6. Semur-en-Auxois

- **Overview**: A fairytale town set high above the Armançon River, Semur-en-Auxois is known for its medieval architecture, fortified walls, and towers. Its cobblestone streets wind through a picturesque old town, where half-timbered houses and charming squares evoke the spirit of medieval Burgundy. The town's dramatic setting, perched on pink granite cliffs, adds to its magical atmosphere.
- **Must-See**: The keep and fortified walls, Church of Notre-Dame, the river promenade.

7. Flavigny-sur-Ozerain

- **Overview**: Flavigny-sur-Ozerain is a stunning medieval village, famous for its historic abbey and for being the filming location of the movie Chocolat. The village is set high on a hill, offering scenic views of the surrounding countryside. Flavigny is also known for producing aniseed-flavored sweets, made at the village's ancient abbey. Narrow streets lined with stone houses and lush gardens make it a delightful place to explore.
- **Must-See**: Abbaye Saint-Pierre, Flavigny candy shop, medieval streets and viewpoints.

8. Noyers-sur-Serein

- **Overview:** Considered one of the most beautiful villages in France, Noyers-sur-Serein is a hidden gem that seems frozen in time. This small village is surrounded by medieval fortifications and boasts charming half-timbered houses, arcaded streets, and scenic squares. The nearby Serein River adds to the peaceful, rustic atmosphere of this quaint village.
- **Must-See**: The village fortifications, local art galleries, the Serein River banks.

9. Tournus

- **Overview**: Located on the banks of the Saône River, Tournus is a small town with a big historical impact, especially known for the Abbey of Saint-Philibert, one of the oldest monastic complexes in France. The town offers riverside charm, Romanesque architecture, and a laid-back atmosphere, making it perfect for exploring on foot. Tournus is also a gateway to Burgundy's southern vineyards.
- **Must-See**: Abbey of Saint-Philibert, the riverfront, local restaurants serving Burgundy specialties.

10. Châteauneuf-en-Auxois

- **Overview:** Overlooking the Burgundy Canal, Châteauneuf-en-Auxois is a medieval village that retains much of its historical character, with stone houses, narrow streets, and a magnificent 12th-century château. From the village, visitors can enjoy panoramic views of the surrounding countryside and canal. It's a great place to explore by foot or as part of a boating tour along the Burgundy Canal.
- **Must-See**: Château de Châteauneuf, canal views, hiking and boating opportunities.

Natural Wonders in Burgundy

Burgundy's landscapes are as diverse and beautiful as its cultural heritage, offering a wide range of natural wonders that captivate outdoor enthusiasts and nature lovers. From lush forests and serene rivers to dramatic rock formations and scenic vineyards, here are some of Burgundy's must-see natural wonders:

1. Morvan Regional Natural Park

- **Overview**: The Morvan is Burgundy's green heart, a vast area of forested hills, lakes, and rivers, offering countless opportunities for hiking, cycling, and water sports. Covering over 285,000 hectares, this natural park is ideal for exploring Burgundy's wildlife and nature. Visitors can enjoy scenic walks through ancient forests, visit the park's lakes for boating and swimming, or hike to panoramic viewpoints.
- **Highlight**s: Lac des Settons (perfect for water sports), Cascade de Gouloux (picturesque waterfall), and hiking trails offering stunning views of the countryside.

2. Rochers du Saussois

- **Overview**: These towering limestone cliffs are a paradise for rock climbers and adventurers, located along the Yonne River near Merry-sur-Yonne. The cliffs rise dramatically above the river, creating an awe-inspiring natural landscape. Even for non-climbers, the Rochers du Saussois offers beautiful views and a peaceful atmosphere, with picnic spots and walking trails nearby.

- **Highlights**: Scenic hikes along the Yonne River, rock climbing for all levels, and panoramic views from the top of the cliffs.

3. Caves of Arcy-sur-Cure

- **Overview:** These prehistoric caves are home to some of the oldest known cave paintings in France, dating back over 28,000 years. The caves, located near the village of Arcy-sur-Cure, are an important archaeological site and a natural wonder, with impressive stalactites, stalagmites, and ancient cave art. Guided tours offer an opportunity to learn about the cave's history and marvel at its natural formations.
- **Highlights**: Ancient cave paintings, fascinating geological formations, and guided tours of the cave system.

4. Vineyards of Côte d'Or

- **Overview**: Burgundy's iconic vineyards, particularly those of Côte de Nuits and Côte de Beaune, are not just a cultural and economic treasure—they are also a natural wonder.

Stretching across rolling hills and fertile valleys, the vineyards create a stunning mosaic of green during the growing season and vibrant reds and yellows in the autumn. The Climats of Burgundy, a UNESCO World Heritage site, showcase the unique terroir that makes Burgundy's wines so special.

- **Highlights**: Scenic vineyard tours, wine tastings, and walking or cycling through the picturesque landscape.

5. Bibracte and Mont Beuvray

- **Overview:** Mont Beuvray is a prominent peak in the Morvan and the site of the ancient Gaulish town of Bibracte. The mountain offers panoramic views of the surrounding forest and is a popular destination for hikers and history enthusiasts. Bibracte, an important archaeological site, was once the capital of the Aedui tribe and played a key role in Julius Caesar's conquest of Gaul. Today, visitors can explore the ruins of the ancient town while enjoying the natural beauty of Mont Beuvray.
- **Highlights**: Hikes to the summit of Mont Beuvray, exploring the ancient ruins of Bibracte, and visiting the on-site archaeological museum.

6. Côte Chalonnaise Vineyards

- **Overview:** Slightly less famous than the Côte d'Or, the Côte Chalonnaise is home to beautiful rolling hills and less crowded, but equally stunning, vineyards. The region is known for producing excellent red and white wines, and its landscape is ideal for scenic drives, cycling, or leisurely walks through the vineyards and charming villages.
- **Highlights**: Wine tours, peaceful countryside walks, and tasting Burgundy's less-known but high-quality wines.

7. Lac de Saint-Agnan

- **Overview:** This peaceful lake, located in the Morvan Regional Natural Park, is a hidden gem, perfect for those looking to escape the crowds. The lake is surrounded by forests and is a popular spot for fishing, swimming, and relaxing by the water. Hiking trails around the lake allow visitors to fully immerse themselves in the natural beauty of the region.
- **Highlights**: Swimming, boating, picnicking, and walking trails around the lake.

Museums and Cultural Sites in Burgundy

Burgundy's rich cultural history is preserved in its many museums and cultural sites, which showcase everything from medieval art and archaeology to wine and local craftsmanship. Here are some of the most notable museums and cultural sites in the region:

1. Musée des Beaux-Arts de Dijon

- **Location**: Dijon
- **Overview**: Housed in the former Palace of the Dukes of Burgundy, this is one of France's most prestigious museums. Its vast collection spans thousands of years, from ancient Egyptian artifacts to Renaissance and modern art. The museum's highlight is the Tombs of the Dukes of Burgundy, remarkable Gothic sculptures that are a must-see for visitors.
- **Highlights**: Tombs of the Dukes of Burgundy, French and European art, and temporary exhibitions.

2. Musée de l'Hôtel-Dieu (Hospices de Beaune)

- **Location**: Beaune
- **Overview**: This historic hospital, founded in 1443, is one of the most iconic buildings in Burgundy. Now a museum, the Hospices de Beaune is famous for its Gothic architecture and its annual wine auction. Inside, visitors can

explore the old hospital wards, pharmacy, and the chapel, as well as see masterpieces like Rogier van der Weyden's The Last Judgment.

- **Highlights**: Gothic architecture, historical hospital exhibits, and The Last Judgment painting.

3. Musée de la Vie Bourguignonne
- **Location:** Dijon
- **Overview**: This museum offers a fascinating look into the daily life and traditions of the people of Burgundy from the 18th century to the present. Housed in a former monastery, the museum displays a wide range of artifacts, including traditional costumes, tools, and recreated 19th-century shops. It provides insight into Burgundy's rich cultural heritage and rural lifestyle.
- **Highlights**: Traditional costumes, recreated historical settings, and rural life exhibits.

4. Musée de Bibracte
- **Location:** Mont Beuvray
- **Overview**: This archaeological museum is dedicated to the ancient Gaulish city of Bibracte, located on Mont Beuvray. The museum showcases the history and archaeology of the Celtic Aedui tribe and their interactions with the

Romans. Visitors can learn about the excavation of Bibracte and explore artifacts that reveal the everyday life of the Gauls.
- **Highlights**: Gaulish artifacts, Roman-era exhibits, and tours of the archaeological site.

5. Musée du Vin de Bourgogne
- **Location**: Beaune
- **Overview**: Dedicated to Burgundy's rich wine-making history, this museum is housed in a beautiful Renaissance building in the heart of Beaune. Visitors can learn about the region's wine-making traditions, viticulture, and the tools and techniques used in wine production over the centuries. The museum also explores the social and cultural impact of wine in Burgundy.
- **Highlights**: Wine-making exhibits, historical wine tools, and local wine history.

6. Musée Alésia
- **Location:** Alise-Sainte-Reine
- **Overview**: Located near the site of the famous Battle of Alésia, where Julius Caesar defeated the Gauls, this museum offers a detailed look at the clash between Roman and Gaulish civilizations. The museum's exhibits include reconstructions of Roman and Gaulish camps, interactive displays, and archaeological artifacts from the battlefield.

- **Highlights**: Roman-Gaulish exhibits, archaeological site tours, and historical reenactments.

7. Musée des Arts Sacrés
- **Location:** Dijon
- **Overview**: Situated in the Church of Sainte-Anne, this museum is dedicated to religious art and artifacts from the region's rich Catholic history. The museum's collection includes liturgical objects, sculptures, paintings, and other works that reflect the deep religious traditions of Burgundy.
- **Highlights**: Religious art, liturgical objects, and Gothic and Renaissance sculptures.

Hidden Gems of Burgundy

While Burgundy is famous for its vineyards and historic cities, it also boasts hidden gems that are lesser-known yet equally captivating. These attractions offer visitors a chance to explore Burgundy's rich history and natural beauty away from the crowds.

1. Château de Bazoches
- **Location:** Bazoches
- **Overview**: A 12th-century castle set in the Morvan countryside, Château de Bazoches is notable for being the residence of Sébastien Le Prestre de Vauban, the famed military engineer of Louis XIV. The château offers guided tours of its richly decorated rooms and exhibits related to Vauban's work in military fortifications. The estate's gardens provide sweeping views of the surrounding area.
- **Highlights**: Vauban's study, medieval architecture, and panoramic views of the Morvan.

2. Grottes de Blanot
- **Location**: Blanot
- **Overview**: The Blanot caves are a hidden underground wonder, located near the village of Blanot. This system of natural limestone caves features impressive stalactites, stalagmites, and

underground lakes. Guided tours take visitors deep into the caves to explore their fascinating geology, offering a tranquil and awe-inspiring experience.

- **Highlights**: Stunning rock formations, crystal-clear underground lakes, and guided tours through the cave system.

3. Château de Sully

- **Location:** Sully
- **Overview**: Often overlooked by travelers, this stunning Renaissance château is a peaceful retreat in the Burgundy countryside. Built in the 16th century, the Château de Sully is beautifully preserved, with a moat, formal gardens, and elegant interiors. The château also hosts art exhibitions and events, making it a lovely stop for history and art enthusiasts.
- **Highlights**: Renaissance architecture, beautifully landscaped gardens, and art exhibitions.

4. Musée de la Résistance en Morvan

- **Location:** Saint-Brisson
- **Overview**: This museum, located in the heart of the Morvan Regional Natural Park, is dedicated to the memory of the French Resistance during World War II. The Morvan was a key center of Resistance activity, and the museum offers

exhibits on the region's role in the war, including artifacts, photos, and personal stories. It's a must-visit for history buffs interested in the lesser-known aspects of WWII.

- **Highlights**: WWII artifacts, moving exhibits on the French Resistance, and peaceful Morvan surroundings.

5. Le Creusot

- **Location:** Le Creusot
- **Overview**: Known for its industrial heritage, Le Creusot is home to Château de la Verrerie, a glass factory turned stately residence. The town played a major role during the Industrial Revolution, and visitors can explore the Ecomusée Creusot Montceau, which tells the story of Burgundy's industrial history through interactive displays. Le Creusot is also a gateway to lesser-known hiking trails and natural parks.
- **Highlights**: Château de la Verrerie, industrial history museum, and nearby hiking trails.

6. Bibracte Museum and Archaeological Site

- **Location:** Mont Beuvray
- **Overview**: Situated on the slopes of Mont Beuvray, Bibracte is the ancient capital of the Aedui tribe, offering a deep dive into Celtic history. Unlike more well-known Roman ruins,

Bibracte is a hidden gem that attracts history enthusiasts looking to explore the remnants of this pre-Roman civilization. The museum features artifacts uncovered during excavations, and the surrounding forests offer scenic hiking opportunities.

- **Highlights**: Archaeological ruins, the Celtic museum, and hikes around Mont Beuvray.

7. Brancion Castle and Village

- **Location**: Brancion
- **Overview**: This small medieval village, perched on a hilltop, feels like stepping back in time. Brancion is home to a 12th-century castle that overlooks the surrounding valleys, and its cobbled streets, ancient church, and breathtaking views make it a charming, lesser-known destination. The village remains largely untouched by modern tourism, making it perfect for visitors seeking peace and history.
- **Highlights**: The castle ruins, Church of Saint-Pierre, and panoramic views of the Burgundy countryside.

Off-the-Beaten-Path Adventures in Burgundy

For travelers seeking more adventure and unique experiences, Burgundy offers a range of exciting off-the-beaten-path activities that allow visitors to explore the region's natural beauty, culture, and history in an unconventional way.

1. Biking Along the Burgundy Canal

- **Location:** Burgundy Canal, various towns
- **Overview**: Stretching for over 240 kilometers, the Burgundy Canal offers a peaceful and scenic cycling route that winds through vineyards, small villages, and historic towns. Visitors can rent bikes and follow the towpath along the canal, stopping at charming locks, riverside cafés, and hidden villages along the way. It's a great way to discover Burgundy at a relaxed pace.
- **Highlights**: Scenic rides through vineyards, visits to lockhouses, and stops at small, authentic villages.

2. Hot Air Ballooning Over Vineyards

- **Location:** Various locations in Burgundy, including Beaune and Chalon-sur-Saône
- **Overview**: For a truly memorable experience, hot air balloon rides over Burgundy's rolling vineyards offer stunning bird's-eye views of the region's countryside. Floating gently above the

vineyards, rivers, and medieval villages at sunrise or sunset, visitors can capture unparalleled panoramic views of the landscape.

- **Highlights**: Views of the vineyards, aerial views of historic châteaux, and an unforgettable adventure.

3. Kayaking in the Morvan

- **Location**: Morvan Regional Natural Park
- **Overview**: The rivers and lakes of the Morvan offer exciting opportunities for kayaking and canoeing. The Cure and Chalaux rivers are popular with adventure seekers due to their fast-moving waters and picturesque surroundings. Visitors can paddle through rapids or enjoy a more relaxed journey on calmer waters, all while being immersed in the Morvan's lush forests.
- **Highlights**: Whitewater kayaking on the Chalaux River, calm paddling on the Cure River, and pristine natural surroundings.

4. Hiking to Roche de Solutré

- **Location:** Near Mâcon
- **Overview**: The Roche de Solutré is a dramatic limestone cliff that rises 493 meters above the vineyards of southern Burgundy. It's a fantastic destination for a hike, offering panoramic views

of the surrounding countryside. The site is also an important archaeological location, with prehistoric artifacts discovered at its base. A hike to the summit rewards adventurers with sweeping vistas of Burgundy's vineyards and the Saône River Valley.

- **Highlights**: Stunning views from the top, fascinating prehistoric history, and hiking through picturesque vineyards.

5. Exploring Burgundy's Cistercian Abbeys

- **Location:** Various locations, including Abbaye de Fontenay and Abbaye de Cîteaux
- **Overview**: For those with an interest in history and architecture, following the Cistercian Abbey Route is a unique way to explore Burgundy. The Cistercian order was born in Burgundy, and visitors can explore lesser-known abbeys such as Cîteaux Abbey, the birthplace of the movement, or the UNESCO-listed Abbaye de Fontenay, set in serene surroundings.
- **Highlights**: Exploring beautiful Romanesque and Gothic architecture, peaceful gardens, and learning about the monastic history of the region.

6. Boating Along the Saône River

- **Location**: Saône River, various towns including Chalon-sur-Saône and Tournus

- **Overview**: Renting a boat to travel along the Saône River offers a tranquil and immersive way to see Burgundy's countryside. Travelers can explore the region's small riverside villages, stop at markets, and enjoy leisurely lunches at waterside restaurants. Boating along the Saône allows for a more relaxed, slow-paced adventure, with opportunities to see Burgundy from a different perspective.
- **Highlights**: Exploring Burgundy by boat, stopping in riverside towns, and peaceful views along the river.

7. Horseback Riding in the Morvan

- **Location:** Morvan Regional Natural Park
- **Overview**: The Morvan's vast forests, meadows, and lakes make it a prime destination for horseback riding adventures. Riders can explore remote trails, ride through the region's scenic landscapes, and experience Burgundy's natural beauty from a different vantage point. Riding tours are available for all levels, from beginners to experienced riders.
- **Highlights**: Riding through lush forests, peaceful lake views, and exploring less-traveled paths in the Morvan.

CHAPTER THREE

Burgundy's Culinary Delights

Food and Wine

Burgundy's Culinary Scene: Signature Foods and Local Products

Burgundy is a gastronomic paradise, renowned for its rich culinary traditions, high-quality local ingredients, and world-famous wines. Whether you're dining at a Michelin-starred restaurant or exploring a village market, Burgundy's food scene offers a mouth-watering array of dishes that reflect the region's deep connection to its land and heritage. Here's a guide to Burgundy's signature foods and must-try local products.

1. Coq au Vin

- **Overview:** Perhaps the most famous dish from Burgundy, Coq au Vin is a traditional French stew made with rooster (or chicken) slow-cooked in Burgundy's red wine, usually Pinot Noir. The dish is flavored with mushrooms, onions, garlic, and lardons (small strips of pork fat), resulting in a hearty and flavorful meal.

- **Best Places to Try**: Most traditional restaurants in Burgundy offer Coq au Vin, particularly in **Beaune** and **Dijon**.

2. Boeuf Bourguignon

- **Overview**: Another iconic dish, Boeuf Bourguignon is a rich beef stew slow-cooked in red wine with carrots, onions, mushrooms, and bacon. It's typically served with mashed potatoes, making it a comforting, hearty meal perfect for colder days. This dish highlights the region's famous red wines, which are used to enhance the flavor of the meat.
- **Best Places to Try**: Look for it in brasseries and traditional French restaurants, especially in cities like Dijon, Beaune, and Autun.

3. Escargots de Bourgogne (Burgundy Snails)

- **Overview:** Burgundy is famous for its snails, which are usually prepared with garlic butter, parsley, and shallots. The snails are often served as an appetizer and are a delicacy in the region. Their distinct taste and texture, combined with the rich garlic butter sauce, make them a must-try for adventurous eaters.
- **Best Places to Try**: Escargots can be found in restaurants across Burgundy, but they are especially popular in the Dijon area.

4. Poulet de Bresse

- **Overview:** A prized poultry product, Poulet de Bresse is a specific breed of chicken from the Bresse region, just east of Burgundy. These chickens are known for their exceptional quality, with tender, flavorful meat. Poulet de Bresse is often roasted or poached, and it's considered one of the finest types of chicken in the world.
- **Best Places to Try**: High-end restaurants in Burgundy, particularly those specializing in fine dining, often feature Poulet de Bresse on their menus.

5. Époisses de Bourgogne (Cheese)

- **Overview:** One of Burgundy's most famous cheeses, Époisses is a soft, pungent cow's milk cheese that is washed in Marc de Bourgogne (a local brandy) during its aging process. The cheese has a creamy texture and a strong aroma, making it a favorite among cheese connoisseurs.
- **Best Places to Try:** Cheese shops and markets across Burgundy, particularly in Dijon and Beaune, will offer Époisses. Many restaurants also include it on their cheese boards.

6. Charolais Beef

- **Overview**: Charolais is a breed of cattle that produces some of the highest-quality beef in

France. Known for its tender texture and rich flavor, Charolais beef is often grilled, roasted, or used in traditional Burgundian dishes like steak frites. The cattle are raised in the Charolais-Brionnais region of southern Burgundy.

- **Best Places to Try:** Steakhouses and bistros throughout Burgundy feature Charolais beef, particularly in areas near Autun and Mâcon.

7. Dijon Mustard

- **Overview:** Burgundy is home to the world-renowned Dijon mustard, which originated in the city of Dijon. Made from brown mustard seeds and white wine or wine vinegar, this mustard is known for its smooth texture and strong, tangy flavor. It's a staple in French kitchens and is used in everything from salad dressings to sauces.

- **Best Places to Try**: You can find Dijon mustard in markets and shops across Burgundy, but for the full experience, visit mustard factories like La Moutarderie Fallot in Beaune, where you can learn about its production and taste different varieties.

8. Pain d'Épices (Gingerbread)

- **Overview**: Pain d'Épices is a traditional French gingerbread, often associated with the city of Dijon. Made with honey, spices, and sometimes nuts or dried fruits, this dense cake is a festive treat, especially around Christmas. Its rich, aromatic flavor makes it a popular snack or dessert in Burgundy.
- **Best Places to Try:** Bakeries and specialty shops in Dijon are the best places to sample this spiced bread.

9. Gougères (Cheese Puffs)

- **Overview**: Gougères are small, savory pastries made from choux dough mixed with cheese, typically Comté or Gruyère. These light, airy puffs are often served as an appetizer or alongside a glass of Burgundy wine. Gougères are a popular snack at wine tastings and make for an elegant yet simple introduction to Burgundian cuisine.
- **Best Places to Try**: Gougères are served in many cafés and wine bars across Burgundy, especially in Beaune and Nuits-Saint-Georges.

10. Crème de Cassis

- **Overview:** A sweet, dark liqueur made from blackcurrants, Crème de Cassis is another

Burgundian specialty. It's famously used to make the Kir, a popular aperitif that combines Crème de Cassis with white wine (often Bourgogne Aligoté). Crème de Cassis is also enjoyed on its own as a digestif or used in desserts.

- **Best Places to Try:** You can find Crème de Cassis in most wine shops in Burgundy, and it's often used in cocktails at restaurants and bars throughout the region.

11. Truffles

- **Overview:** Burgundy is home to its own variety of black truffles, known as Tuber uncinatum. These truffles are highly prized for their earthy aroma and rich flavor, often used in fine dining to enhance dishes like pastas, risottos, and meats. The Burgundy truffle season runs from September to December, and many restaurants offer special menus featuring this delicacy during this time.
- **Best Places to Try:** Truffle dishes are commonly served in upscale restaurants across Burgundy, and you can also join truffle hunts in areas like Nuits-Saint-Georges.

12. Burgundy Wine

- **Overview:** No discussion of Burgundy's culinary scene is complete without mentioning its world-famous wines. Burgundy is home to some of the finest vineyards in the world, particularly known for its Pinot Noir and Chardonnay varieties. The region's wines are often enjoyed alongside meals, with different appellations offering unique flavor profiles.

- **Best Places to Try**: Wine tastings are available throughout Burgundy, with top spots including Beaune, Nuits-Saint-Georges, and Chablis. Many vineyards offer tours and tastings, allowing visitors to sample a range of wines directly from the producers.

Wine Regions and Tasting Tours in Burgundy

Burgundy is world-renowned for its exceptional wines, particularly Pinot Noir and Chardonnay. The region's unique combination of climate, soil, and centuries of winemaking expertise has made it a top destination for wine lovers. Burgundy is divided into several key wine regions, each with its own distinct character and appellations. Visitors can explore these regions through guided wine tours, tastings at family-owned vineyards, and visits to historic wine cellars.

1. Côte de Nuits

- **Location:** North of Beaune, from Marsannay to Nuits-Saint-Georges

- **Overview**: Known as the heart of Burgundy's Pinot Noir production, Côte de Nuits is home to some of the most prestigious red wines in the world, including those from Gevrey-Chambertin, Vosne-Romanée, and Nuits-Saint-Georges. The vineyards here produce rich, complex wines that are often described as earthy, with notes of dark fruit and spices.
- **Top Vineyards to Visit:** Domaine de la Romanée-Conti, Domaine Armand Rousseau, Domaine Dujac
- **Wine Tasting Experience**: Visitors can enjoy tastings at some of the world's most famous vineyards, often by appointment. Many wineries offer guided tours through their vineyards and cellars, providing insight into the meticulous winemaking process.

2. Côte de Beaune
- **Location**: South of Beaune, from Ladoix-Serrigny to Santenay
- **Overview**: While the Côte de Beaune is also known for its excellent red wines, it's particularly famous for its Chardonnay. The Meursault, Puligny-Montrachet, and Chassagne-Montrachet vineyards produce some of the finest white wines in the world. These wines are known for their

buttery, mineral-driven flavors and aging potential.
- **Top Vineyards to Visit:** Domaine Leflaive, Domaine des Comtes Lafon, Château de Meursault
- **Wine Tasting Experience:** Many vineyards in Côte de Beaune offer tastings with a focus on white wines. You'll find opportunities to sample aged wines alongside freshly bottled vintages, as well as food pairings featuring local cheeses and charcuterie.

3. Côte Chalonnaise
- **Location:** South of Côte de Beaune, around Chalon-sur-Saône
- **Overview**: Known for producing high-quality wines at more accessible prices, the Côte Chalonnaise is a great region for discovering both Pinot Noir and Chardonnay without the exclusivity of other areas. Villages like Mercurey, Givry, and Rully offer wines that are vibrant and elegant, with strong fruit-forward characteristics.
- **Top Vineyards to Visit**: Domaine Faiveley, Domaine Michel Juillot, Château de Chamirey
- **Wine Tasting Experience**: Visitors can enjoy more informal and relaxed tastings here, often with vineyard owners or winemakers themselves. Many vineyards are family-run, offering a

personal touch and deep knowledge of local wine traditions.

4. Mâconnais

- **Location:** Southernmost Burgundy, around Mâcon
- **Overview**: The Mâconnais region is best known for its Chardonnay, which is typically more affordable and approachable than the wines from Côte de Beaune. The wines are fresh, floral, and fruit-driven, with notable appellations like Pouilly-Fuissé, Saint-Véran, and Mâcon-Villages. This region is less formal, making it ideal for casual wine enthusiasts.
- **Top Vineyards to Visit**: Domaine Ferret, Domaine des Héritiers du Comte Lafon, Domaine Saumaize-Michelin.
- **Wine Tasting Experience**: Mâconnais offers scenic vineyard tours with tastings that focus on vibrant, fresh white wines. It's a more laid-back experience, often including outdoor tastings in picturesque vineyards.

5. Chablis

- **Location:** Northern Burgundy, near Auxerre
- **Overview**: Chablis is Burgundy's northernmost wine region and is famous for its steely, mineral-driven Chardonnay. The cool climate

here results in crisp, acidic wines that have become some of the most sought-after whites in the world. Chablis Grand Cru and Premier Cru vineyards produce the finest examples of these wines.

- **Top Vineyards to Visit:** Domaine William Fèvre, Domaine Jean-Paul & Benoît Droin, Domaine Laroche
- **Wine Tasting Experience**: Tastings in Chablis focus on the purity of the Chardonnay grape, often accompanied by tours of the region's limestone-rich vineyards. Many wineries offer comparative tastings between their Grand Cru and Premier Cru wines.

Wine Etiquette and Tips for Visitors

When visiting Burgundy's vineyards and participating in wine tastings, understanding local wine etiquette can enhance your experience and help you make the most of your visit. Here are some tips for wine enthusiasts:

1. Make Appointments for Tastings

Many Burgundy vineyards, especially the prestigious ones, require appointments for tastings. Plan ahead by booking your visits in advance, especially during peak tourist seasons (spring and harvest time in September/October).

2. Be Respectful of Traditions

Burgundy's winemaking culture is deeply rooted in tradition. While tastings are usually casual, it's essential to show respect for the winemakers, their craft, and the vineyard's heritage. Engage with hosts by asking questions about the wines, terroir, and production methods.

3. Proper Wine Tasting Technique

When tasting wine, follow these basic steps:

- Look: Observe the wine's color and clarity.
- Smell: Swirl the glass gently to release aromas, then take a deep sniff.
- Taste: Sip the wine, let it roll around your mouth to appreciate its flavors, then swallow or spit (especially if visiting multiple vineyards).
- Discuss: Feel free to share your impressions, but avoid overly critical comments, as winemakers take pride in their work.

4. Take Notes

With so many wines to sample, it's a good idea to take notes on the wines you taste. Whether it's your favorite bottle, flavor profiles, or interesting facts, keeping a record will help you remember and find wines to purchase later.

5. Dress Comfortably but Appropriately

Wine tasting is often a casual affair, but it's still best to dress in smart-casual attire. Wear comfortable shoes, especially if you plan to tour the vineyards. If you're visiting in summer, bring a hat and sunscreen, as vineyard tours can involve outdoor walking.

6. Avoid Wearing Strong Perfumes

Since wine tasting is all about aromas, it's important not to wear strong perfumes or colognes that might interfere with the scent of the wine. This allows you to fully appreciate the subtle aromas of each glass.

7. Ask Before Taking Photos

While most vineyards are happy for visitors to take photos, it's courteous to ask first, especially if you're in the production areas or private cellars. Some places may prefer discretion due to privacy or intellectual property concerns.

8. Learn the Wine Terminology

Familiarizing yourself with basic wine terminology can enhance your tasting experience. Burgundy wines are often categorized by their terroir, including Grand Cru and Premier Cru designations, which indicate the quality and prestige of the vineyard.

9. Purchase Wine as a Souvenir

After a tasting, consider buying a bottle or two to take home. Many vineyards offer wines that are not available for export, making this a unique opportunity to taste and purchase rare wines. Most vineyards can ship bottles internationally if you can't carry them yourself.

10. Explore Wine Shops and Local Markets

In addition to vineyard visits, Burgundy has numerous wine shops and local markets where you can sample and purchase wines from smaller producers. Many of these shops offer expert advice on pairing wines with regional dishes.

CHAPTER FOUR

Accommodation and Practical

Travel Information

Accommodation Options

Luxury Hotels, Boutique Stays, Budget Options, and Farm Stays in Burgundy

Burgundy offers a wide range of accommodations to suit every traveler's needs, from opulent luxury hotels and charming boutique stays to budget-friendly options and authentic farm stays. Whether you're looking for five-star comfort, a cozy countryside retreat, or an immersive farm experience, Burgundy has something for everyone.

1. Luxury Hotels

Burgundy boasts several world-class luxury hotels that offer top-notch service, fine dining, and opulent accommodations. These hotels often feature elegant surroundings, including vineyards, châteaux, or historic buildings.

Hôtel Le Cep (Beaune)

- **Overview:** A 5-star hotel located in the heart of Beaune, Hôtel Le Cep offers refined elegance with spacious suites and personalized services. It features a renowned spa and is within walking distance of the Hospices de Beaune and local vineyards.

- **Contact**: +33 3 80 22 35 48 | Website: www.hotel-cep-beaune.com

Château de Gilly (Gilly-lès-Cîteaux)

- **Overview:** A historic 14th-century castle turned luxury hotel, Château de Gilly offers guests the chance to experience royal treatment in grand rooms with antique furnishings. The hotel is surrounded by gardens and vineyards, with a gourmet restaurant on-site.
- **Contact**: +33 3 80 62 89 98 | Website: www.grandesetapes.fr

Hôtel Les Deux Chevres (Gevrey-Chambertin)

- **Overview**: Located in a picturesque wine village, this boutique luxury hotel offers stunning vineyard views, personalized service, and beautifully designed rooms. The hotel specializes in wine tours and tastings.
- **Contact**: +33 6 71 18 20 65 | Website: www.lesdeuxchevres.com

2. Boutique Stays

Burgundy's boutique hotels offer intimate and unique experiences with personalized service and locally inspired design. These smaller properties often emphasize the charm and authenticity of the region.

La Maison d'Olivier Leflaive (Puligny-Montrachet)

- **Overview**: This boutique hotel, set in the heart of a vineyard, combines modern luxury with traditional charm. The hotel offers wine tours, tastings, and even winemaker dinners, making it an ideal choice for wine lovers.
- **Contact**: +33 3 80 21 95 27 | Website: www.olivier-leflaive.com

La Cueillette (Meursault)

- **Overview**: A beautiful boutique hotel housed in a 19th-century château, La Cueillette offers a peaceful retreat with luxurious spa treatments, gourmet dining, and elegant rooms. It's located in the heart of Burgundy's wine region.
- **Contact**: +33 3 80 20 62 80 | Website: www.lacueillette.com

Hostellerie Le Cèdre (Beaune)

- **Overview**: Situated in a former mansion, this charming boutique hotel combines historic architecture with modern luxury. With an on-site gourmet restaurant, wine cellar, and lush garden, it's a perfect blend of comfort and style.

- **Contact**: +33 3 80 24 01 01 | Website: www.lecedre-beaune.com

3. Budget Options

For travelers looking to experience Burgundy without breaking the bank, there are plenty of budget-friendly accommodations that provide comfort and convenience without sacrificing quality.

Hotel ibis Styles Beaune Centre (Beaune)
- **Overview**: A modern and budget-friendly hotel located in the heart of Beaune, close to popular attractions like the Hospices de Beaune. The hotel offers bright, comfortable rooms with free breakfast and Wi-Fi.
- **Contact**: +33 3 80 20 88 88 | Website: www.accorhotels.com

Hotel des Remparts (Dijon)
- **Overview**: Located in Dijon's historic center, this affordable hotel offers charming, rustic rooms with easy access to the city's main attractions. Perfect for budget-conscious travelers who want a central location.
- **Contact**: +33 3 80 30 48 52 | Website: www.hotel-remparts-dijon.com

Hotel Athanor (Beaune)

- **Overview**: A cozy and affordable hotel located in the center of Beaune's historic district. Hotel Athanor offers clean, comfortable rooms with a traditional ambiance, perfect for budget travelers exploring the wine capital.
- **Contact**: +33 3 80 24 09 20 | Website: www.hotelathanor.com

4. Farm Stays

For a more immersive experience, Burgundy offers numerous gîtes and farm stays that give travelers a taste of rural life. These accommodations often come with rustic charm, home-cooked meals, and a chance to connect with the local culture.

Ferme de la Lochère (Marigny-lès-Reullée)

- **Overview**: Located in the peaceful countryside, Ferme de la Lochère is a traditional Burgundian farm that offers cozy accommodations with the opportunity to participate in farm activities like grape harvesting and cheese making.
- **Contact**: +33 6 85 60 32 88 | Website: www.fermedelalochere.com

Domaine de la Pierre Ronde (Sombernon)

- **Overview**: Set on a biodynamic farm, Domaine de la Pierre Ronde offers unique accommodations, including eco-friendly yurts and farm tours. Guests can enjoy nature walks, local produce, and a true farm-to-table experience.
- **Contact**: +33 3 80 49 77 43 | Website: www.pierre-ronde.com

Le Pré Germain (Beurizot)

- **Overview**: This charming farmhouse offers a quiet escape in the Burgundian countryside, with comfortable rooms, organic meals, and the chance to explore nearby villages and nature reserves.
- **Contact**: +33 3 80 64 66 98 | Website: www.pre-germain.com

Recommended Hotels in Burgundy

Here is a curated selection of the best hotels across different categories, from luxury accommodations to boutique stays and budget-friendly options, each with contact details for easy booking.

1. Luxury Hotels

1.1 Hôtel Le Cep

- **Location:** Beaune
- **Description**: A prestigious 5-star hotel located in the heart of Burgundy's wine capital, Beaune. This historical property offers opulent rooms, a Michelin-starred restaurant, and a luxurious spa.
- **Facilities**: Spa, wine cellar, gourmet dining, and private gardens.
- **Contact**:
    - Phone: +33 3 80 22 35 48
    - Email: info@hotel-le-cep.com
    - Website: www.hotel-le-cep.com
    - Address: 27 Rue Maufoux, 21200 Beaune, France

1.2 Château de Gilly

- **Location:** Vougeot
- **Description**: A stunning castle converted into a luxury hotel, nestled between Dijon and Beaune. This hotel offers an authentic historical

experience with elegant rooms, a fine dining restaurant, and beautiful gardens.

- **Facilities**: Outdoor pool, restaurant, and extensive wine cellar.
- **Contact**:
  - Phone: +33 3 80 62 89 98
  - Email: contact@chateau-gilly.com
  - Website: www.chateau-gilly.com
  - Address: Gilly-lès-Cîteaux, 21640 Vougeot, France

2. Boutique Stays

2.1 La Maison d'Olivier Leflaive

- **Location**: Puligny-Montrachet
- **Description**: A charming boutique hotel owned by renowned winemaker Olivier Leflaive. This hotel offers wine tours and tastings as part of the experience, along with stylish rooms and a cozy atmosphere.
- **Facilities**: Wine tasting, restaurant, and vineyard tours.
- **Contact**:
  - Phone: +33 3 80 21 95 27
  - Email: info@maison-olivierleflaive.fr
  - Website: www.maison-olivierleflaive.fr
  - Address: Place du Monument, 21190 Puligny-Montrachet, France

2.2 Hôtel des Remparts

- **Location**: Beaune
- **Description**: A beautiful boutique hotel set in a former 17th-century mansion. Hôtel des Remparts offers intimate accommodations with unique decor and an excellent location close to Beaune's historic center.
- **Facilities**: Garden, bar, and free Wi-Fi.
- **Contact**:
  - Phone: +33 3 80 24 94 94
  - Email: contact@hoteldesremparts.com
  - Website: www.hoteldesremparts.com
  - Address: 48 Rue Thiers, 21200 Beaune, France

3. Budget-Friendly Hotels

3.1 Ibis Styles Dijon Central

- **Location**: Dijon
- **Description**: A modern and affordable hotel located in the center of Dijon. It's ideal for travelers on a budget, offering comfortable rooms and excellent access to Dijon's cultural attractions.
- **Facilities**: Free breakfast, Wi-Fi, and family rooms.
- **Contact**:
  - Phone: +33 3 80 30 44 00
  - Email: h0852@accor.com

- Website: www.ibis.com
- Address: 3 Place Grangier, 21000 Dijon, France

3.2 Kyriad Hotel Beaune

- **Location**: Beaune
- **Description**: This budget-friendly hotel offers cozy rooms, excellent service, and is located just outside the Beaune city center, providing easy access to both the city and surrounding vineyards.
- **Facilities**: Restaurant, free parking, and Wi-Fi.
- **Contact**:
  - Phone: +33 3 80 22 74 10
  - Email: beaune@kyriad.fr
  - Website: www.kyriad.com
  - Address: 10 Route de Montagny, 21200 Beaune, France

4. Farm Stays and Unique Experiences

4.1 La Ferme de la Lochère

- **Location:** Marigny-le-Cahouët
- **Description**: A charming farm stay that allows guests to experience rural life in Burgundy. Set in the rolling countryside, the property offers comfortable rooms, farm-to-table dining, and local farm tours.

- **Facilities**: Farm activities, local produce, and restaurant.
- **Contact**:
  - **Phone**: +33 3 80 96 58 59
  - **Email**: info@fermedelalochere.fr
  - **Website**: www.fermedelalochere.fr
  - **Address**: 7 Rue du Parc, 21150 Marigny-le-Cahouët, France

4.2 Château de Bresse-sur-Grosne

- **Location**: Bresse-sur-Grosne
- **Description**: Stay in a beautifully restored 18th-century château surrounded by scenic countryside. The château offers luxurious accommodations with a historical twist, including access to gardens, hiking trails, and nearby attractions.
- **Facilities**: Hiking, historical tours, and breakfast service.
- **Contact**:
  - Phone: +33 3 85 49 12 43
  - Email: info@chateaubresse.com
  - Website: www.chateaubresse.com
  - Address: 4 Route du Château, 71460 Bresse-sur-Grosne, France

Travel Essentials

Banks, ATMs, and Financial Services in Burgundy (2025)

When traveling in Burgundy, tourists will find a wide range of banking services, ATMs, and financial facilities to make their stay convenient and secure. From large international banks to local institutions, visitors have access to all the essential financial services they may need during their travels.

1. Major Banks in Burgundy

1.1 BNP Paribas

- **Overview:** One of the largest international banks in France, BNP Paribas offers a wide range of services, including currency exchange, ATM access, and international transfers.
- **Branches in Burgundy**:
    - Dijon: 17 Rue des Forges, 21000 Dijon
    - Beaune: 6 Boulevard Jules Ferry, 21200 Beaune
    - Phone: +33 820 82 00 01
    - Website: www.bnpparibas.fr

1.2 Crédit Agricole

- **Overview**: Crédit Agricole is a popular bank in rural and suburban areas of France, making it one of the most accessible in Burgundy. It offers

ATMs, credit services, and cash withdrawal facilities for international travelers.

- **Branches in Burgundy**:
    - Dijon: 12 Place du Président Wilson, 21000 Dijon
    - Autun: 21 Avenue Charles de Gaulle, 71400 Autun
    - Phone: +33 3 80 60 80 60
    - Website: www.credit-agricole.fr

1.3 Société Générale

- **Overview:** A well-known French bank with extensive ATM and branch networks throughout Burgundy. Services include international transfers, ATM withdrawals, and foreign currency exchange.
- **Branches in Burgundy:**
    - Beaune: 1 Place de la Halle, 21200 Beaune
    - Dijon: 42 Rue de la Liberté, 21000 Dijon
    - Phone: +33 3 80 50 50 50
    - Website: www.societegenerale.fr

1.4 La Banque Postale

- **Overview**: As a branch the French postal service, La Banque Postale offers banking and postal services throughout Burgundy. It is ideal for basic banking services, including ATM withdrawals, bill payments, and transfers.

- **Branches in Burgundy**:
    - Auxerre: 9 Rue du Temple, 89000 Auxerre
    - Chalon-sur-Saône: 14 Quai des Messageries, 71100 Chalon-sur-Saône
    - Phone: +33 3 80 92 80 80
    - Website: www.labanquepostale.fr

2. ATM Availability

ATMs (Distributeurs Automatiques de Billets) are widely available in Burgundy, especially in larger cities like Dijon, Beaune, and Chalon-sur-Saône. Most ATMs accept international credit and debit cards, including Visa, MasterCard, and Maestro. It is recommended to use ATMs associated with major banks to avoid higher fees.

ATM Locations:

- City Centers: Major cities like Dijon and Beaune have ATMs at almost every corner, particularly near tourist attractions, banks, and shopping areas.
- Supermarkets: Large supermarket chains such as Carrefour and E. Leclerc often have ATMs on site.

- Train Stations: All major train stations in Burgundy, including Dijon-Ville Station and Beaune Station, have 24-hour ATMs.

Tips for Using ATMs in Burgundy:
- Check if your home bank has a partnership with any French banks to avoid extra withdrawal fees.
- Always choose to be charged in the local currency (EUR) to get a better exchange rate.
- Keep an eye on daily withdrawal limits, as they may differ depending on your card's country of issue.

3. Currency Exchange

Although ATMs are the most convenient way to access euros, travelers can also exchange foreign currency at banks, exchange bureaus, or even at some larger hotels. Below are some options for currency exchange in Burgundy:

- **BNP Paribas and Société Générale:** Many branches offer currency exchange services at the counter. Ensure you have your passport for verification.

- **Travelex**: Travelex operates exchange counters in major airports, including Lyon–Saint-Exupéry Airport and Paris Charles de Gaulle Airport, which are close to Burgundy for travelers arriving internationally.

- **Beaune Tourism Office**: While not offering exchange services, the Beaune Tourist Office can direct travelers to local exchange points and provide assistance with financial services.

- **Dijon Currency Exchange**: Located near Dijon Ville Station, this dedicated currency exchange shop offers competitive rates for most major currencies.

4. Credit Card Usage and Payment Tips

Credit and debit cards are widely accepted throughout Burgundy, especially in larger towns and tourist areas. However, smaller villages, independent stores, and markets may prefer cash, so it's advisable to carry some euros for smaller purchases. When paying by card:

- **Credit Cards Accepted**: Visa and MasterCard are the most commonly accepted, with American Express accepted at fewer locations. Contactless payments are becoming more common.
- **Cash and Contactless:** In restaurants and shops, contactless payments for amounts up to €50 are frequently accepted. However, for larger transactions, you will need to enter your PIN.

5. Traveler's Checks

Traveler's checks are not commonly used or accepted in France, including Burgundy. If you have traveler's checks, your best bet is to exchange them for euros at a bank or currency exchange office. However, ATMs and credit cards are generally more convenient and offer better exchange rates.

6. Emergency Financial Services

In case you encounter any financial emergencies, such as lost or stolen credit cards, here are some key contact numbers:

- Visa Emergency Assistance: +33 1 42 77 45 45
- MasterCard Global Service: +33 1 45 67 84 84
- American Express Global Assist: +33 1 47 77 72 00
- Lost or Stolen Cards: Contact your issuing bank immediately. French banks typically offer a 24-hour hotline for card cancellations.

Local Laws, Customs, and Language Tips for Burgundy Travelers

Understanding the local laws, customs, and language can significantly enhance your experience when visiting Burgundy. Below is a comprehensive guide to help you navigate the region's regulations, traditions, and etiquette, ensuring a smooth and enjoyable stay.

1. Local Laws and Regulations

Burgundy, like the rest of France, operates under French national laws. While these laws are straightforward, it's important to be aware of key regulations that may impact tourists:

1.1. Drinking Age and Alcohol Laws

- The legal drinking age in France is 18. Minors are not allowed to purchase or consume alcohol in public spaces.
- Alcohol consumption is generally permitted in restaurants, bars, and public areas like parks, but be mindful of local rules, especially in family-friendly spaces.
- Drunk driving is taken seriously in France. The legal blood alcohol limit is 0.05% (50 mg of alcohol per 100 ml of blood) for drivers, and 0.02% for those with less than three years of driving experience.

1.2. Smoking

- Smoking is prohibited in enclosed public spaces, including restaurants, bars, public transport, and government buildings.
- Designated smoking areas are available in some outdoor spaces, including terraces at cafés and restaurants.

1.3. Respect for Heritage Sites

- Many of Burgundy's attractions are UNESCO World Heritage sites or historical landmarks. Damaging, defacing, or littering in these areas can result in heavy fines.
- Follow the guidelines provided at museums, castles, and religious sites. In some cases, photography may be restricted, especially in sacred or fragile environments.

1.4. Drug Laws

- All recreational drugs are illegal in France, and penalties for possession, use, or distribution are severe.
- Travelers should also be cautious when bringing prescription medications into France. Ensure you carry them in their original packaging and with a prescription.

1.5. Driving Laws

- Drive on the right-hand side of the road. Seat belts are mandatory for all passengers.
- The speed limit is 130 km/h (about 80 mph) on highways, 80-90 km/h on rural roads, and 50 km/h in urban areas. Traffic cameras are prevalent, and speeding fines can be steep.

2. Local Customs and Etiquette

Burgundy has its own charm and culture, deeply rooted in history and traditions. To enjoy the best of this region, it helps to be mindful of local customs:

2.1. Greeting Etiquette

- A typical greeting is a "Bonjour" (Good day) or "Bonsoir" (Good evening), accompanied by a smile or nod.
- The French custom of "la bise" (cheek kisses) is common among friends but not expected with strangers or in formal settings. A handshake is more common when meeting someone for the first time.

2.2. Dining Etiquette

- Meals are an important part of French culture, and dining out is a leisurely affair. Avoid rushing through meals, and enjoy each course.

- In restaurants, tipping is not obligatory, as a 15% service charge is usually included in the bill. However, rounding up or leaving small change (5-10%) as a tip for good service is appreciated.
- Wine tasting is a popular activity in Burgundy. It's polite to listen carefully to the winegrower's explanation of the wines and to avoid rushing through a tasting session.

2.3. Church Etiquette
- Burgundy is home to many historic churches and cathedrals. When visiting religious sites, dress modestly, particularly in rural areas. Avoid loud conversations and respect areas designated for prayer.
- Be sure to follow any instructions regarding photography or restricted areas, as some sections of religious buildings may be closed to tourists.

2.4. Market Etiquette
- Weekly farmers' markets are common in Burgundy's towns and villages. It's polite to greet vendors with a friendly "Bonjour" before purchasing anything.
- Bargaining is not customary at markets. Prices are generally fixed, though it's common to be offered a small discount if buying in bulk or being a loyal customer.

3. Language Tips

While many locals in Burgundy may speak some English, especially in tourist areas, a few French phrases will go a long way in improving your interactions and enhancing your experience:

3.1. Common French Phrases for Travelers

Bonjour / Bonsoir – Hello / Good evening

Merci – Thank you

S'il vous plaît – Please

Pardon / Excusez-moi – Excuse me / Sorry

Parlez-vous anglais? – Do you speak English?

Où est… ? – Where is… ?

Combien ça coûte ? – How much does it cost?

Je voudrais… – I would like…

3.2. Numbers for Basic Transactions

- Un (1), Deux (2), Trois (3), Quatre (4), Cinq (5) – Essential for small purchases and ordering food or drinks.

3.3. Polite Phrases

- The French value politeness. Always say "Bonjour" when entering a shop or speaking to someone, and use "Merci" when leaving or after receiving help.
- "S'il vous plaît" is a must when asking for something, and it's considered more polite to

phrase questions indirectly. For example, "I would like a coffee" (Je voudrais un café) is better received than "Give me a coffee" (Donnez-moi un café).

3.4. Signs and Notices
- Ouvert – Open
- Fermé – Closed
- Entrée – Entrance
- Sortie – Exit
- Toilettes – Restrooms

4. Cultural Traditions to Observe
Burgundy has a rich tapestry of traditions and festivals. Learning about them can add depth to your trip:

4.1. Wine Harvest Festival (Fête des Vendanges)
- Held in autumn, this is one of the most celebrated events in Burgundy. It's a time of celebration in wine-producing villages, marked by feasts, music, and dancing. Join in the fun and be sure to sample the Beaujolais Nouveau, the first wine of the season.

4.2. Saint Vincent Tournante
- An annual wine festival held in honor of Saint Vincent, the patron saint of winegrowers. Each year, a different village hosts the event, which

includes a procession, wine tastings, and various festivities.

4.3. Christmas Markets

- During the holiday season, many towns, including Dijon and Beaune, host traditional Christmas markets (Marché de Noël). These markets feature local crafts, gourmet foods, and mulled wine, creating a magical holiday atmosphere.

Health, Safety, and Travel Insurance for Visiting Burgundy

Ensuring you are well-prepared in terms of health, safety, and insurance before your visit to Burgundy will help you enjoy a worry-free trip. This guide covers everything from health precautions and safety tips to the importance of travel insurance for a stress-free stay.

1. Health Services in Burgundy

1.1. Public Healthcare System (Sécurité Sociale)

France has one of the best healthcare systems in the world. Visitors from EU countries can access public healthcare services through the European Health Insurance Card (EHIC) or the Global Health Insurance Card (GHIC). If you're from a non-EU country, you may need to pay upfront for treatment and claim reimbursement later through your insurance provider.

Hospitals: There are several well-equipped hospitals in Burgundy's main cities:

- **Centre Hospitalier Universitaire (CHU) Dijon**
    - 14 Rue Gaffarel, 21000 Dijon
    - Phone: +33 3 80 29 30 31

- **Centre Hospitalier de Beaune**
    - Rue des Chaumes, 21200 Beaune
    - Phone: +33 3 80 24 44 44

1.2. Pharmacies

Pharmacies are readily available across Burgundy and are easily identified by the green cross sign. Many towns have a 24-hour pharmacy on rotation, called a "pharmacie de garde". Pharmacists can provide over-the-counter medications, advice, and assistance with minor ailments.

- **Tip**: It's advisable to bring a small first-aid kit with essentials like painkillers, plasters, and any personal medications, especially if you're planning on exploring rural areas.

2. Vaccinations and Health Precautions

Before traveling to Burgundy, it's recommended to check the latest health guidelines from your local travel advisory. Generally, no special vaccinations are required for France, but you should be up to date on routine vaccinations such as:

- Tetanus
- Measles, Mumps, and Rubella (MMR)
- Influenza (if traveling during flu season)

2.1. Tick-borne Diseases

If you plan on hiking or spending time in wooded areas, be aware that tick bites in some parts of France can transmit Lyme disease. Always wear protective clothing and use tick repellents when in rural or forested areas. Check yourself for ticks after outdoor activities and seek medical advice if you notice a bite or rash.

3. Travel Insurance

3.1. Why You Need Travel Insurance

Having comprehensive travel insurance is essential to cover any unforeseen medical expenses, cancellations, or disruptions to your trip. France has excellent medical care, but without insurance, costs can add up, especially for non-EU travelers who will need to pay upfront for many services.

3.2. What Should Travel Insurance Cover? When choosing travel insurance for Burgundy, ensure your policy includes:

- **Medical expenses**: Coverage for any hospital stays, doctor visits, prescriptions, or medical emergencies.
- **Emergency evacuation**: In the unlikely event that you need emergency transport or repatriation.
- **Trip cancellation or interruption**: Coverage for lost deposits, prepaid expenses, or changes due to unforeseen events.
- **Lost or stolen luggage and personal items**: Ensure valuables, such as cameras or phones, are covered in case of theft or damage.
- **Accidents during adventure activities**: If you plan on hiking, cycling, or participating in other adventurous activities, check that your policy covers these activities.

4. Safety in Burgundy
4.1. General Safety Tips
Burgundy is generally a safe region, with low crime rates in both rural and urban areas. However, as with any destination, it's wise to take basic precautions:

- **Pickpocketing**: While rare, pickpocketing can occur in crowded tourist areas, particularly in markets or near popular landmarks. Keep your belongings secure, use money belts, and be mindful of your surroundings.

- **Valuables**: Avoid carrying large amounts of cash. Use hotel safes for storing passports and valuables.
- **Solo Travel**: Burgundy is a welcoming destination for solo travelers, but be cautious if hiking alone in remote areas. Always inform someone of your route and expected return.

4.2. Emergency Numbers

In case of an emergency, you can contact the following French services:

- Emergency Medical Services (SAMU): Dial 15
- Police: Dial 17
- Fire and Rescue: Dial 18
- European Emergency Number: Dial 112 (works for any emergency in the EU)
- SOS Doctors: +33 826 46 56 56 (for urgent, non-hospital medical care)

4.3. Medical Assistance for Tourists

If you require medical assistance but it's not an emergency, many hotels and tourist offices can recommend local English-speaking doctors. There are also several clinics and urgent care centers in Dijon and other major towns.

5. Safety During Adventure Activities

For adventure seekers, Burgundy offers a variety of outdoor activities, such as hiking, cycling, and hot air ballooning. Ensure you stay safe by following these tips:

- **Hiking**: Burgundy's forests and trails are well-maintained, but always stay on marked paths and carry a map or GPS. Check the weather forecast before venturing out and bring plenty of water and snacks.
- **Cycling**: Burgundy is known for its cycling routes, especially through vineyards. Always wear a helmet, follow road rules, and use reflective gear if cycling during early morning or evening hours.
- **Water Safety**: For canoeing or any water sports on Burgundy's rivers, ensure you wear a life jacket and check the water conditions beforehand.

6. COVID-19 and Other Health Alerts

As of 2025, it's important to stay informed about any global or regional health concerns. Although COVID-19 restrictions have eased, it's a good idea to:

- **Carry proof of vaccination** if required for certain venues or activities.

- **Follow local guidelines**: Mask mandates, hand sanitizers, and social distancing rules may still be in place in certain areas, such as museums or public transportation.

Check the official government website or travel advisory before departure for the latest updates.

CHAPTER FIVE

Transportation and Getting Around Burgundy

Transportation

Getting to Burgundy: Airlines, Trains, and Buses

Burgundy is a well-connected region in central-eastern France, making it accessible from various parts of Europe and the world. Whether you're flying in, arriving by train, or opting for a scenic bus journey, this guide will help you plan your trip to Burgundy with ease.

1. Arriving by Air: Airlines Serving Burgundy

Although Burgundy doesn't have its own major international airport, several nearby airports provide easy access to the region. These airports are well-connected with international airlines and offer convenient transport options to Burgundy.

1.1. Paris Charles de Gaulle (CDG) Airport
- **Location:** Approximately 300 km (186 miles) north of Dijon, the capital of Burgundy.
- **Airlines**: Major international carriers such as Air France, British Airways, Lufthansa, Delta, and Emirates serve CDG.

- **Getting to Burgundy:**
  - **Train:** High-speed TGV trains connect CDG Airport directly to Dijon in about 1.5 hours.
  - **Bus**: Long-distance bus services, such as FlixBus, offer affordable connections from Paris to various towns in Burgundy.
  - **Car**: Renting a car is a popular option for exploring Burgundy's countryside. The drive from CDG to Dijon takes about 3 hours via the A6 highway.

1.2. Lyon-Saint Exupéry Airport (LYS)

- **Location**: About 200 km (124 miles) south of Dijon.
- **Airlines**: Airlines such as Air France, KLM, easyJet, and Ryanair operate flights to LYS from across Europe and beyond.
- **Getting to Burgundy:**
  - **Train**: Direct TGV trains from Lyon-Saint Exupéry Airport to Dijon take around 1.5 hours.
  - **Car**: Driving from Lyon to Burgundy takes roughly 2 hours, and rental cars are readily available at the airport.

1.3. Geneva Airport (GVA), Switzerland

- **Location:** Around 150 km (93 miles) southeast of Dijon.

- **Airlines**: Geneva Airport is served by Swiss Air, British Airways, easyJet, and many other international airlines.
- **Getting to Burgundy:**
  - ○ **Train**: Regular train services run from Geneva to Dijon, taking approximately 2 hours.
  - ○ **Car**: Driving from Geneva to Dijon takes about 2 hours via the A40 and A39 highways.

1.4. Paris Orly Airport (ORY)

- **Location**: South of Paris, around 260 km (161 miles) from Dijon.
- **Airlines**: Orly serves domestic and European flights, including low-cost carriers like Transavia and Vueling.
- **Getting to Burgundy:**
  - ○ **Train:** Shuttle services connect Orly to Paris Gare de Lyon, where you can catch a TGV to Burgundy.
  - ○ **Bus**: FlixBus and other long-distance buses connect Orly Airport with Burgundy's main towns.
  - ○ **Car**: A direct drive from Orly to Burgundy takes around 2.5 hours.

2. Arriving by Train: TGV and Regional Services

France's high-speed rail network makes train travel one of the most efficient and comfortable ways to reach Burgundy. The region's central location and well-connected rail system ensure easy access from major cities across France and Europe.

2.1. TGV (Train à Grande Vitesse)

The TGV is France's high-speed train service, offering fast connections between Burgundy and cities such as Paris, Lyon, and Marseille. Dijon is the main hub for TGV services in Burgundy, but other towns such as Beaune, Mâcon, and Chalon-sur-Saône are also well-served.

- **From Paris:** TGV trains from Paris Gare de Lyon to Dijon take about 1.5 hours. Trains also run to Beaune and Chalon-sur-Saône, making it convenient for exploring the wine regions.
- **From Lyon**: TGV trains from Lyon Part-Dieu to Dijon take around 1.5 hours.
- **From Geneva**: Direct trains from Geneva to Dijon take around 2 hours.

2.2. TER (Transport Express Régional)

For shorter regional journeys or exploring smaller towns, the TER train service is an excellent option. TER trains connect towns within Burgundy and link them with nearby regions.

- **Dijon to Beaune**: A 20-minute TER journey.
- **Dijon to Auxerre**: About 2 hours by TER, offering scenic views along the way.
- **Dijon to Mâcon**: About 1 hour, with several trains per day.

2.3. International Trains

For travelers coming from neighboring countries, Burgundy is accessible via international train services:

- **Eurostar**: Connects London to Paris, where you can transfer to a TGV bound for Burgundy.
- **TGV Lyria:** Direct trains from Geneva and Zurich to Dijon.

3. Arriving by Bus: Long-Distance Coaches

If you're looking for a more budget-friendly travel option, long-distance bus services provide a comfortable and affordable way to reach Burgundy from various European cities.

3.1. FlixBus

FlixBus offers frequent services from major cities like Paris, Lyon, and Geneva to towns in Burgundy such as

Dijon, Beaune, and Chalon-sur-Saône. Tickets can be booked online in advance for lower fares, and buses offer amenities such as free Wi-Fi and reclining seats.

- **Paris to Dijon**: About 4-5 hours by bus.
- **Lyon to Beaune**: Approximately 2.5 hours by bus.
- **Geneva to Dijon**: Around 3 hours by bus.

3.2. BlaBlaCar Bus

BlaBlaCar Bus (formerly Ouibus) is another long-distance coach service with routes connecting Burgundy to cities across France and neighboring countries.

- **Lille to Dijon:** A 6-hour journey, passing through Paris.
- **Marseille to Dijon**: Around 5-6 hours, with buses available throughout the day.

4. Driving to Burgundy: By Car

For those who prefer the flexibility of a road trip, driving to Burgundy is a popular option, especially if you're traveling from nearby regions or countries. The region's well-maintained highways offer scenic routes through vineyards, rolling hills, and charming villages.

4.1. From Paris

- **Distance**: 300 km (186 miles)
- **Route**: Take the A6 motorway (Autoroute du Soleil) south from Paris towards Lyon, which passes through Burgundy.
- **Travel Time**: About 3 hours, depending on traffic.

4.2. From Lyon

- **Distance**: 200 km (124 miles)
- **Route**: The A6 motorway connects Lyon with Burgundy. You can take scenic detours through wine regions like Beaujolais.
- **Travel Time**: Around 2 hours by car.

4.3. Car Rentals

Car rentals are available at all major airports and train stations, offering a great way to explore Burgundy's countryside and hidden gems. Some popular rental companies include Avis, Hertz, Europcar, and Sixt.

5. Local Transportation in Burgundy

Once you arrive in Burgundy, getting around is easy with a variety of local transport options:

- **Trains**: Regional TER trains connect towns and cities across Burgundy, making it easy to explore the region without a car.

- **Buses**: Local buses operate in towns like Dijon, Beaune, and Auxerre, with regular services to key tourist destinations.
- **Taxis and Ride-Sharing**: Taxis are available in major towns, and ride-sharing apps like Uber operate in larger cities like Dijon.
- **Cycling**: Burgundy is known for its cycling routes, especially along the Voie des Vignes, a scenic path that passes through vineyards and picturesque villages.

Car Rentals, Bicycle Rentals, and Local Transportation Options in Burgundy

Once you arrive in Burgundy, having reliable transportation is essential for exploring the region's picturesque vineyards, historic towns, and scenic countryside. This guide covers everything you need to know about car rentals, bicycle rentals, and other local transportation options to help you get around Burgundy comfortably and efficiently.

1. Car Rentals in Burgundy

Renting a car is one of the best ways to explore Burgundy, especially if you plan on visiting smaller villages, wineries, or natural attractions in more rural areas. The region's roads are well-maintained, offering beautiful drives through the countryside and easy access to hidden gems.

1.1. Major Car Rental Companies

Car rental services are available at airports, train stations, and major cities like Dijon, Beaune, and Chalon-sur-Saône. Popular international car rental agencies include:

- Avis
- Hertz
- Europcar
- Sixt
- Enterprise Rent-A-Car

1.2. Rental Locations

- **Dijon:** Rental agencies are available at Gare de Dijon Ville (Dijon Train Station) and in the city center.
- **Beaune**: You'll find several car rental services near the Beaune Train Station and in the town center.
- **Lyon and Paris Airports**: If you're flying into Burgundy through Lyon-Saint Exupéry or Paris airports, renting a car directly from the airport is a convenient option.

1.3. Requirements for Renting a Car
- **Driver's License:** A valid driver's license is required. If you're from outside the EU, you may need an International Driving Permit (IDP).
- **Age Requirements**: Most car rental agencies require drivers to be at least 21 years old, and there may be additional fees for drivers under 25.
- **Insurance**: Basic insurance is typically included, but it's advisable to check the coverage details and consider additional options for more comprehensive protection.

1.4. Tips for Driving in Burgundy
- **Speed Limits:** 50 km/h (31 mph) in towns, 90 km/h (56 mph) on country roads, and 130 km/h (81 mph) on highways.
- **Toll Roads**: The A6 motorway, which connects Paris and Lyon via Burgundy, has tolls. Be sure to have a credit card or cash for toll booths.
- **Parking**: Most towns have ample parking, including public lots. In smaller villages, free parking is often available. Always check local signs for parking rules.

2. Bicycle Rentals and Cycling in Burgundy
Burgundy is a paradise for cyclists, offering numerous well-marked cycling paths through vineyards, rolling hills, and quaint villages. Whether you're interested in

short rides or multi-day cycling tours, renting a bicycle is a fantastic way to experience the region's natural beauty.

2.1. Popular Cycling Routes

- **La Voie des Vignes (The Vineyard Way):** A scenic cycling path that runs through Burgundy's wine country, connecting towns like Beaune, Nuits-Saint-Georges, and Santenay.
- **La Voie Verte (The Green Way):** A longer cycling route that stretches across Burgundy, offering peaceful rides through forests, along canals, and through small villages.

2.2. Bicycle Rental Companies

Bicycle rentals are widely available in tourist towns, and some hotels and guesthouses offer bike rentals to guests. Some popular options include:

- **Dijon à Vélo**: Bike rentals in Dijon, with a variety of options including electric bikes.
- **Bourgogne Evasion**: Specializes in bike rentals and guided cycling tours around Beaune and the Côte d'Or wine region.
- **CycloRando**: Offers a range of bikes, including electric and hybrid bikes, in various towns in Burgundy.

2.3. Types of Bicycles Available

- **Standard Bicycles**: Perfect for leisurely rides through towns and vineyards.
- **Electric Bikes (E-Bikes):** A popular option for tackling Burgundy's hills and longer distances.
- **Hybrid and Mountain Bikes**: Great for off-road trails and more challenging rides through the countryside.

2.4. Cycling Safety Tips

- **Helmet**: Helmets are recommended, especially for longer rides and on more challenging terrain.
- **Bike Paths**: Stay on designated cycling paths and respect local traffic rules when riding on public roads.
- **Maps and Navigation**: Many routes are well-marked, but carrying a map or using a GPS app will help you stay on course.

3. Local Transportation Options

Burgundy's towns and cities offer various local transportation options, from public buses to taxis and ride-sharing services, making it easy to get around without a car.

3.1. Buses

Regional buses operated by Mobigo provide reliable connections between towns and cities in Burgundy. You can travel from Dijon to Beaune, Auxerre, Chalon-sur-Saône, and other destinations by bus.

- **Mobigo Bus Routes**: Buses cover key tourist areas and are ideal for traveling between towns when you don't have a car.
- **Schedules and Tickets:** Bus schedules vary by route, and tickets can be purchased at stations, on board, or online via the Mobigo website.

3.2. Taxis

Taxis are available in major towns like Dijon and Beaune and can be booked in advance or hailed at taxi stands.

- Taxi Dijon: +33 3 80 41 41 12
- Taxi Beaune: +33 3 80 22 22 22

3.3. Ride-Sharing Services

While services like Uber are not as widely available in rural areas, they do operate in larger cities like Dijon. BlaBlaCar, a popular ride-sharing app in France, is a great option for longer-distance travel, especially if you're heading to smaller towns or less touristy areas.

3.4. Trams and Urban Transportation in Dijon

Dijon is the only city in Burgundy with a tram system. The Dijon Tramway offers two lines (T1 and T2) that connect the city center with key destinations, including the Dijon Ville Train Station and the University of Burgundy.

- **Tickets**: Tickets for the tram can be purchased at stations or through the local public transport app. They are also valid for buses within Dijon.

4. Scenic Alternatives: Boats and Hot Air Balloons

For a more adventurous and unique way to explore Burgundy, consider alternative forms of transportation, such as:

4.1. Canal Cruises

Burgundy is home to several beautiful canals, including the Canal de Bourgogne, which winds through the heart of the region. Canal cruises are a peaceful and scenic way to experience Burgundy, especially if you want to slow down and take in the sights.

- **Self-Drive Boat Rentals**: Companies like Le Boat and Locaboat Holidays offer houseboat rentals, allowing you to cruise Burgundy's canals at your own pace.
- **Guided Cruises:** For a more relaxed experience, you can join a guided canal cruise with stops at wineries, historic sites, and charming villages.

4.2. Hot Air Balloon Rides

For a bird's-eye view of Burgundy's vineyards and castles, hot air ballooning is an unforgettable experience.

- **Burgundy Montgolfière**: A company offering hot air balloon rides over the vineyards and historic towns of Burgundy, typically around Beaune and Chalon-sur-Saône.
- **Flight Time**: Rides usually last about 1-1.5 hours, with options to take off during sunrise or sunset for the most breathtaking views.

Driving Tips and Directions to Tourist Centers in Burgundy

Driving in Burgundy offers a fantastic opportunity to explore the region's charming villages, picturesque vineyards, and stunning landscapes. This guide provides essential driving tips and directions to key tourist centers, ensuring a smooth and enjoyable journey through this beautiful part of France.

1. Driving Tips for Burgundy

1.1. Road Rules and Regulations

Speed Limits:

- In towns: 50 km/h (31 mph)
- Open roads: 90 km/h (56 mph)
- Highways: 130 km/h (81 mph), reduced to 110 km/h (68 mph) in wet conditions.
- Alcohol Limit: The legal blood alcohol limit is 0.05%. It's advisable to avoid drinking altogether if you plan to drive.

Roundabouts: Traffic in roundabouts flows counter-clockwise. Yield to vehicles already in the roundabout.

1.2. Parking

- **On-Street Parking**: Look for designated parking spaces. Pay attention to parking signs to avoid fines. Blue zones usually require a parking disc (available at tourist offices or shops).

- **Public Parking Lots**: Most towns have public parking areas, often marked with a sign showing a "P." Some larger cities, like Dijon, have underground parking garages.
- **Rural Areas**: In small villages, parking is generally free and readily available near attractions.

1.3. Navigation

- **GPS and Maps:** Using a GPS or a navigation app like Google Maps will help you find your way around. Offline maps are also useful in areas with poor mobile signal.
- **Signage**: Road signs are generally clear, but it's good to familiarize yourself with French road signs before you arrive.

1.4. Scenic Drives

- **Route des Grands Crus**: This scenic route takes you through Burgundy's famous wine-producing areas, offering stunning views of vineyards and charming villages.
- **Burgundy Canal**: The roads parallel to the canal provide beautiful scenery and opportunities to stop at small villages along the way.

Here are directions to some of the must-visit tourist centers in Burgundy, along with key attractions in each area.

2.1. Dijon

From Paris: Take the A6 motorway south. The drive takes about 3 hours (300 km).

Key Attractions:

- **Palace of the Dukes**: A historical landmark and museum.
- **Dijon Market (Les Halles):** A vibrant market to sample local produce.
- **Owl's Trail (La Chouette):** A walking route with 22 owl statues marking the path to key sites.

2.2. Beaune

From Dijon: Take the A31 motorway south for about 45 minutes (45 km).

Key Attractions:

- **Hôtel-Dieu**: A historic hospital with stunning architecture.
- **Wine Tours:** Explore the nearby vineyards and taste world-renowned wines.
- **Beaune Market**: Held on Saturdays, showcasing local products.

2.3. Chalon-sur-Saône

From Dijon: Take the A6 south and then A36 east for about 1 hour (70 km).

Key Attractions:

- Musée Nicéphore Niépce: A museum dedicated to photography.
- **Saint Vincent Cathedral**: A beautiful example of Gothic architecture.
- **River Saône**: Scenic walks along the riverbank.

2.4. Autun

From Dijon: Take the N80 west for about 1 hour (90 km).

Key Attractions:

- **Roman Theater**: One of the best-preserved Roman theaters in France.
- **Cathedral of Saint-Lazare**: An architectural masterpiece.
- **Historic City Walls**: Explore remnants of the ancient city walls.

2.5. Mâcon

From Lyon: Take the A6 south for about 1 hour (70 km).

Key Attractions:

- **Saint Vincent Cathedral**: A beautiful church with rich history.

- **Mâcon Wine Tours**: Discover the wine culture of southern Burgundy.
- **The Lamartine Museum**: Dedicated to the poet Alphonse de Lamartine.

2.6. Cluny

From Mâcon: Take the D981 north for about 30 minutes (35 km).

Key Attractions:
- **Cluny Abbey**: Once the largest church in the world and a significant historical site.
- **National Museum of Medieval Art**: Showcasing artifacts from the abbey.

3. Safety Considerations

3.1. Wildlife

When driving in rural areas, be cautious of wildlife crossing roads, particularly at dawn and dusk.

3.2. Weather Conditions

Check the weather forecast before heading out, as rain and fog can affect driving conditions. Always adjust your speed accordingly.

3.3. Emergency Numbers

Keep emergency contact numbers handy:
- Emergency Services: 112 (general emergency)
- Police: 17

- Fire Department: 18

Maps and Navigation in Burgundy

Navigating Burgundy's beautiful landscapes, charming towns, and historic sites is made easier with the right maps and navigation tools. This guide covers the best options for finding your way around the region, whether you prefer digital maps or traditional paper guides.

1. Digital Maps and Navigation Apps

1.1. Google Maps

- **Overview:** A highly reliable tool for driving, walking, and public transport directions.
- **Features**: Real-time traffic updates, estimated travel times, satellite view, and user reviews for attractions.
- **Offline Access**: You can download specific areas for offline navigation, which is useful in regions with spotty mobile coverage.

1.2. Waze

- **Overview:** A community-driven navigation app that provides real-time traffic updates.
- **Features**: Alerts about traffic jams, road closures, and police checkpoints.
- **User Interaction**: Users can report issues, making it effective for avoiding delays.

1.3. Citymapper
- **Overview:** Particularly useful for public transportation navigation.
- **Features**: Offers detailed transit options, including buses and trains, and provides real-time updates.
- **Coverage**: While primarily focused on urban areas, it can help navigate larger towns like Dijon.

1.4. Maps.me
- **Overview:** An offline map application that provides detailed hiking, biking, and walking paths.
- **Features**: Ideal for discovering off-the-beaten-path attractions and routes.
- **Offline Functionality**: Download maps for specific areas and access them without internet.

2. Traditional Maps and Guides
2.1. Paper Road Maps
- **Availability**: You can find detailed road maps of Burgundy at tourist information centers, gas stations, and bookstores in the region.
- **Advantages**: Useful for planning routes in areas with poor mobile signal and for offline reference.

2.2. Guidebooks

- **Overview:** Travel guidebooks, such as those from Lonely Planet or Rick Steves, offer curated information on attractions, dining, and accommodation.
- **Maps Included**: Many guidebooks feature maps and suggested itineraries to enhance your travel experience.

3. Local Navigation Resources

3.1. Tourist Information Centers

- **Location:** Most towns in Burgundy, including Dijon, Beaune, and Chalon-sur-Saône, have tourist information centers.
- **Services**: They provide free maps, brochures, and personalized recommendations for exploring the area.

3.2. Signage

- **Road Signs**: Burgundy has clear signage for major tourist attractions and directions to nearby towns.
- **Walking Trails**: Look for markers along hiking and cycling paths, which indicate distances and points of interest.

4.1. Planning Ahead

Before setting out, review your route and identify any key stops or attractions along the way. This is especially useful in rural areas where GPS may not always have the latest information.

4.2. Backup Options

Always have a backup navigation option, such as a printed map or guidebook, in case your digital device fails or loses signal.

4.3. Language Considerations

While many signs are in French, major tourist attractions often have English translations. Familiarizing yourself with basic French road signs can be helpful.

4.4. Keep Your Device Charged

Ensure your phone or GPS device is fully charged before starting your journey. Consider carrying a portable charger for longer trips.

CHAPTER SIX

Burgundy's Culture and Traditions

Customs and Traditions

Festivals and Events in Burgundy
Burgundy is rich in cultural and historical traditions, with festivals and events celebrated throughout the year. These festivities are a wonderful way to experience the region's vibrant heritage, local customs, and, of course, world-renowned food and wine.

1. Wine Festivals

1.1. Les Trois Glorieuses de Bourgogne (The Three Glorious Days)

- **Location:** Beaune
- **Date**: Mid-November 2025 (Exact dates to be confirmed)
- **Overview**: This three-day event is one of Burgundy's most famous festivals, celebrating its prestigious wines. It features the Hospices de Beaune Wine Auction, grand feasts, and wine tastings.
- **Activities**: Wine tastings, gourmet dinners, vineyard tours, and the famous auction that

attracts wine lovers and collectors from around the world.

1.2. Saint-Vincent Tournante

- **Location:** Various wine-growing villages
- **Date**: January 25-26, 2025
- **Overview**: Dedicated to Saint Vincent, the patron saint of winemakers, this event rotates between different Burgundy villages each year. It includes a procession, blessing of the wine, and lively celebrations with wine tastings.
- **Activities**: Local parades, vineyard tours, wine tastings, and traditional Burgundian meals.

2. Cultural and Historical Events

2.1. Medieval Festival in Guédelon

- **Location:** Guédelon Castle
- **Date**: August 2025
- **Overview**: The annual medieval festival at Guédelon Castle, where artisans and craftsmen continue the construction of a medieval castle using 13th-century techniques. The festival brings the Middle Ages to life with costumed re-enactors, traditional crafts, and medieval music.
- **Activities**: Live demonstrations, guided tours, medieval games, and performances.

2.2. Fêtes de la Saint-Jean

- **Location:** Dijon
- **Date**: June 24, 2025
- **Overview**: A celebration of Saint John the Baptist with a mixture of religious and pagan traditions. Bonfires, folk dancing, and music fill the streets, especially in smaller villages.
- **Activities**: Traditional dances, bonfires, and local markets.

3. Music and Arts Festivals

3.1. Festival International d'Opéra Baroque de Beaune

- **Location**: Beaune
- Date: July 2025
- **Overview**: A prestigious event for lovers of classical and baroque opera, held in the stunning backdrop of Hôtel-Dieu and Beaune's ancient churches.
- **Activities**: Performances by world-renowned opera singers and orchestras in historic venues.

3.2. Jazz à Beaune

- **Location**: Beaune
- **Date**: October 2025
- **Overview**: This festival blends jazz music with wine tastings, providing an atmospheric

experience in one of Burgundy's most picturesque towns.

- **Activities**: Jazz concerts, wine tastings, and vineyard tours.

Social Etiquette, Religious Practices, and Cultural Behavior in Burgundy

Burgundy is known for its strong sense of tradition, community, and respect for cultural norms. Understanding and observing local etiquette will help visitors immerse themselves in the Burgundian way of life.

1. Social Etiquette

1.1. Greetings and Politeness

- **Greetings**: When meeting someone, a polite "Bonjour" (Good day) is expected. Handshakes are common in formal settings, while close acquaintances may exchange kisses on the cheek (usually two, one on each side).
- **Titles**: Address people as Monsieur (Mr.) or Madame (Mrs.), especially in formal or professional situations. Using titles demonstrates respect.
- **Politeness**: Always say "s'il vous plaît" (please) and "merci" (thank you) when interacting in restaurants, shops, or any public setting.

1.2. Dining Etiquette

- **Dining Culture**: Meals in Burgundy, especially dinner, are often slow and social. It's common to linger over food, savoring every course.
- **Tipping**: Tipping in restaurants is not obligatory as service is usually included in the bill (marked "service compris"). However, leaving small change or rounding up the bill is appreciated for exceptional service.

1.3. Dress Code

- **Dress Appropriately**: The French, including Burgundians, generally dress well, even for casual outings. In cities like Dijon, it's common to see smart casual attire. When visiting religious sites, it's advisable to dress modestly.
- **Vineyard Visits:** For wine tours and outdoor activities, comfortable yet stylish clothing is common. Be sure to wear sturdy shoes if walking through vineyards.

2. Religious Practices

2.1. Catholic Traditions

- **Catholicism:** As with much of France, Burgundy has a strong Catholic tradition. Churches are central to community life, and religious festivals, such as Saint-Vincent Tournante and Fêtes de la Saint-Jean, are widely observed.

- **Mass Attendance**: If visiting a church during a service, it's important to remain respectful and quiet. Dress modestly and remove hats before entering.

2.2. Church Visits

- **Open to Tourists**: Most churches and cathedrals in Burgundy are open to visitors, though donations are appreciated. Be mindful when taking photos—ask for permission if unsure, especially during services.

3. Cultural Behavior

3.1. Wine Culture

- **Respect for Wine**: Burgundy is world-famous for its wine, and winemaking is taken very seriously. When participating in wine tastings, it's polite to show interest and ask questions. Avoid excessive drinking, as wine is appreciated more for quality than quantity.

- **Wine Etiquette**: Swirl, sniff, and taste—each part of the process is important in Burgundy's wine culture. If visiting a vineyard or attending a tasting, remember to show appreciation for the craft behind the wines.

3.2. Quietness and Respect

- **Quiet Manners:** Burgundians tend to value a certain degree of formality and quietness, especially in public settings like museums, restaurants, and small towns. Loud conversations in restaurants or public transport are generally discouraged.

3.3. Respecting Traditions

- **Traditional Celebrations:** Many rural areas hold onto centuries-old traditions. If you're invited to join a local celebration, do so respectfully, and follow the lead of the locals.
- **Market Etiquette**: In weekly markets, it's polite to greet vendors with a "bonjour" before making any purchases or inquiries. Handling produce is often discouraged unless you're invited to do so by the vendor.

4. Key Phrases to Know

Here are a few key French phrases that can help you navigate cultural situations more smoothly:

- **Bonjour/Bonsoir**: Good day/Good evening
- **S'il vous plaît**: Please
- **Merci**: Thank you

- **Excusez-moi**: Excuse me
- **Parlez-vous anglais?:** Do you speak English?
- **Je ne parle pas bien français**: I don't speak French well
- **Santé!:** Cheers (used when drinking wine or toasting)

Local Customs in Burgundy: Tipping, Greetings, and Dress Code

Understanding and respecting local customs is key to blending in and enjoying a smooth visit to Burgundy. From tipping etiquette to greetings and dress codes, these insights will help you navigate the social and cultural norms of the region.

1. Tipping Etiquette in Burgundy

1.1. Restaurants and Cafés

- **Service Included**: In France, and particularly in Burgundy, restaurant bills typically include a service charge ("service compris"). This means that tipping is not obligatory. However, it is customary to leave a small tip if the service has been particularly good.

- **How Much to Tip**:
  - For excellent service, leaving 5-10% of the total bill is appreciated.

- Alternatively, rounding up the bill or leaving some small change (around €1-€5 depending on the type of meal) is a common gesture.

1.2. Taxis

- **Taxi Tipping**: Tipping taxi drivers is not mandatory, but rounding up to the nearest euro is appreciated.
  - **Example**: If your fare is €18.50, rounding it up to €20 would be a polite gesture.

1.3. Hotels and Accommodation

- **Hotel Staff:**
  - It's common to tip hotel staff, such as porters, who assist with luggage. A tip of €1-€2 per bag is appropriate.
  - For housekeeping, leaving €1-€2 per day is a nice way to show appreciation, especially for longer stays.

- **Concierge**: If a concierge has provided particularly helpful service, such as making dinner reservations or organizing special tours, a tip of €5-€10 is appreciated.

1.4. Tour Guides and Drivers

For guided tours, it is customary to tip around €5-€10 per person for a half-day tour and €10-€20 for a full-day tour if you are satisfied with the service.

2. Greetings and Social Interactions

2.1. Formal and Informal Greetings

- **Bonjour / Bonsoir**: A polite "bonjour" (good day) or "bonsoir" (good evening) is expected when entering a shop, café, or meeting someone for the first time, regardless of the formality of the setting.
    - **Tip**: Always greet shopkeepers or service staff before asking for help; it's considered impolite to skip this formality.

- **Handshakes**: A handshake is the standard greeting in more formal or professional situations, such as when meeting someone for the first time or in business settings. The handshake is usually quick and light.

2.2. La Bise (Cheek Kissing)

- **Cheek Kissing**: Among friends and close acquaintances, the French custom of "la bise" (cheek kisses) is common. In Burgundy, this typically involves two light kisses, one on each cheek.

- o **When to Use:** Only use this greeting when you know the person fairly well. If you're unsure, wait for the other person to initiate.

2.3. Politeness

- **Titles and Address:** Addressing people with Monsieur (Mr.) or Madame (Mrs.) is considered polite, especially in formal situations. When unsure of how formal the interaction is, using titles is always a safe bet.
- **Goodbyes**: When leaving a shop, café, or social gathering, it's customary to say "au revoir" (goodbye) or "bonne journée" (have a nice day).

3. Dress Code in Burgundy

3.1. General Style

- **Smart Casual**: Burgundy, like much of France, values elegance and simplicity in clothing. Even in casual settings, it's common for locals to dress stylishly. Jeans are acceptable, but they are often paired with a smart top, jacket, or scarf.

- **Daytime Attire**:
  - o For sightseeing and general activities during the day, smart casual is the norm.

This could mean tailored pants or neat jeans with a blouse or a collared shirt.

○ Comfortable walking shoes are essential, especially if you plan to explore vineyards or historic villages with cobblestone streets.

3.2. Dining Out and Evening Wear

- **Restaurants**: If dining at a more upscale restaurant or attending a wine-tasting event, dress slightly more formally. Men may wear a jacket, while women might opt for a nice dress or tailored outfit.

- **Events**: For special events like wine festivals or cultural events, locals tend to dress up, so wearing something stylish and semi-formal is recommended.

3.3. Religious Sites

- **Dress Modestly**: When visiting churches or religious sites, modest dress is appreciated. This means avoiding revealing clothing such as shorts, sleeveless tops, or overly short skirts. Covering shoulders and legs, especially for women, is advisable.

3.4. Outdoor Activities

- **Vineyard Visits**: If you're visiting Burgundy's vineyards or engaging in outdoor activities, comfortable clothing and sturdy shoes are important. Bring layers, as the weather can change quickly.
- **Hiking or Biking**: If you plan on hiking or biking, be sure to wear appropriate outdoor gear, including comfortable shoes, sun protection, and a rain jacket if needed.

Adventure and Outdoor Activities

Hiking, Cycling, and Water Sports in Burgundy

Burgundy's scenic landscape offers plenty of opportunities for outdoor enthusiasts to explore its natural beauty. Whether you're into hiking, cycling, or water sports, the region has diverse options to suit different skill levels and preferences.

1. Hiking in Burgundy

Burgundy is blessed with an abundance of trails that take you through vineyards, forests, riversides, and historic villages.

1.1. Wine Trail Walks

- **Route des Grands Crus**: One of the most famous routes, this trail runs through some of Burgundy's most prestigious vineyards, passing through towns like Beaune, Gevrey-Chambertin, and Nuits-Saint-Georges. It's a moderate walk with beautiful views of vineyards and châteaux.

- **Distance**: Varies, with shorter routes around 10 km and longer routes up to 30 km.
- **Difficulty**: Easy to moderate, suitable for most fitness levels.

1.2. Morvan Regional Natural Park

- **Location:** Morvan, an hour's drive from Dijon.
- **Overview**: This rugged, forested area is a haven for hikers. Trails here range from easy nature walks to more challenging routes.
- **Notable Trails**:
    - **Grande Randonnée 13 (GR 13):** A long-distance trail that passes through the Morvan, offering views of lakes, forests, and rolling hills.
    - **Sentier des Crêtes**: A 15 km trail offering panoramic views of the park's highest peaks.

- **Difficulty**: Easy to difficult, depending on the trail.

1.3. Gorges de l'Areuse

- **Location:** Near the town of Vincelles.

- **Overview**: A dramatic gorge with picturesque walking paths along the river. The trail features waterfalls, lush greenery, and rustic bridges.
- **Distance**: Approx. 12 km round trip.
- **Difficulty**: Moderate, with some steep inclines.

2. Cycling in Burgundy

Burgundy is one of France's most popular regions for cycling, with scenic routes that cater to both casual cyclists and experienced bikers.

2.1. The Burgundy Canal (Canal de Bourgogne)
- **Location:** Runs from Dijon to Migennes.
- **Overview**: A flat, easy cycling route that follows the towpaths along the Canal de Bourgogne. Ideal for families or leisurely cyclists, this path passes by vineyards, charming villages, and historic sites.
- **Distance**: The full length of the canal is 242 km, but shorter segments can be explored.
- **Difficulty**: Easy, mostly flat terrain suitable for all levels.

2.2. Voie des Vignes
- **Location:** From Beaune to Santenay.

- **Overview**: This beautiful cycling route takes you through some of Burgundy's most famous vineyards, making it perfect for wine lovers. Stop by local wineries for tastings along the way.
- **Distance**: 21 km.
- **Difficulty**: Moderate, with a few gentle hills.

2.3. Cycling in the Morvan
- **Location:** Morvan Regional Natural Park.
- **Overview**: For those seeking a more challenging ride, the Morvan offers hilly terrain and forested paths. The routes range from beginner to advanced, with some steep climbs for more experienced cyclists.
- **Notable Routes:**
    - **Tour du Morvan**: A 200 km circular route that takes you through the heart of the park.
    - **Mountain Bike Trails**: Several marked trails are available for mountain biking enthusiasts.

- **Difficulty**: Moderate to difficult, depending on the trail.

3. Water Sports in Burgundy

Burgundy's lakes and rivers offer a variety of water sports for those looking to cool off and enjoy the region from a different perspective.

3.1. Canoeing and Kayaking

- **Rivers**: The Cure, Yonne, and Loire rivers are popular spots for kayaking and canoeing.

- **Notable Locations**:
    - **Canoe the Cure River**: Paddle through the Morvan Regional Natural Park and experience the region's serene landscapes.
    - **Yonne River**: Perfect for a leisurely ride, offering scenic views of rolling hills and vineyards.

- **Difficulty**: Easy to moderate, with calm waters suitable for beginners.

3.2. Sailing and Windsurfing

- **Lac des Settons**: Located in the Morvan, this large lake is ideal for sailing and windsurfing.
- **Facilities**: The lake has a marina with boat rentals and windsurfing schools for beginners.
- **Difficulty**: Easy to moderate.

3.3. Paddleboarding

- **Lac de Panthier**: A peaceful lake near Pouilly-en-Auxois, perfect for stand-up paddleboarding (SUP). Rentals are available on-site.
- **Difficulty**: Easy, suitable for all levels.

Hot Air Balloon Rides and Nature Walks in Burgundy

For a more relaxed way of exploring Burgundy's picturesque countryside, consider a hot air balloon ride or a leisurely nature walk.

1. Hot Air Balloon Rides

Hot air ballooning is one of the most unique ways to experience Burgundy's vineyards, castles, and rolling hills from above.

1.1. Overview

- **Locations**: Balloon rides are available from several locations across Burgundy, including Beaune, Dijon, and Chalon-sur-Saône.
- **Highlights**: Float over famous wine regions like Côte de Nuits and Côte de Beaune, spotting historic castles, picturesque villages, and endless vineyards.

- **Duration**: Most flights last between 1-1.5 hours, with the full experience (including setup and landing) lasting about 3 hours.
- **Best Time**: Early morning or late afternoon when winds are calm and the lighting is best for photography.

1.2. Companies Offering Rides

- **Montgolfières de Bourgogne**: One of the premier hot air balloon companies in the region, offering rides over vineyards and the countryside.
- **France Montgolfières:** Another well-established company that offers scenic rides over Burgundy's historic sites and natural landscapes.

2. Nature Walks in Burgundy

For those who prefer exploring on foot at a more leisurely pace, Burgundy offers a range of nature walks.

2.1. Forest of Fontainebleau

- **Location**: Near Vézelay, a UNESCO World Heritage Site.
- **Overview**: This forested area is perfect for a peaceful nature walk, with marked trails that wind through ancient woodlands and past historic sites.

- **Distance**: Various trails ranging from 5 km to 15 km.
- **Difficulty**: Easy to moderate, suitable for families and casual walkers.

2.2. Parc de l'Auxois

- **Location:** Near Arnay-le-Duc.
- **Overview**: A beautiful nature park with walking trails, animal enclosures, and picnic areas. Ideal for families or anyone looking for a relaxing day outdoors.
- **Activities**: Walking, picnicking, and wildlife viewing.

2.3. Sentier des Roches (Path of Rocks)

- **Location**: Near Saulieu, in the Morvan region.
- **Overview**: This trail offers stunning views of rock formations, wooded areas, and panoramic vistas of the surrounding countryside.
- **Distance**: 8 km loop.
- **Difficulty**: Moderate, with some rocky and uneven terrain.

Exploring Burgundy's Wildlife and Landscapes

Burgundy is a region of diverse and captivating natural beauty, featuring everything from rolling vineyards to dense forests and scenic waterways. For nature lovers, it's an exceptional destination where you can experience unique wildlife and landscapes, ranging from the wild forests of the Morvan to peaceful rivers teeming with life.

1. Morvan Regional Natural Park: A Biodiversity Haven

The Morvan Regional Natural Park is Burgundy's crown jewel when it comes to natural beauty and wildlife diversity. Located in the heart of the region, this park offers a mix of forests, rivers, lakes, and hilly terrain, making it an ideal place to explore nature.

1.1. Forests and Woodlands

- **Flora**: The park is home to beech, oak, and pine forests. In spring and summer, the forest floors are carpeted with wildflowers such as orchids, anemones, and primroses.
- **Wildlife**: The forests shelter a variety of animals, including wild boar, roe deer, foxes, and badgers. Birdwatchers will find an abundance of species, including hawks, eagles, and the rare black woodpecker.

1.2. Lakes and Rivers

- **Lac des Settons**: One of the most popular spots in the Morvan, Lac des Settons is a serene lake surrounded by woodlands, ideal for boating, fishing, or simply relaxing. It's also home to otters, frogs, and various species of freshwater fish.
- **Rivers**: The Cure and Yonne rivers wind through the park, providing habitats for herons, kingfishers, and beavers.

1.3. Hiking and Wildlife Viewing

- **Sentier du Tacot**: This popular trail takes you through the heart of the Morvan, offering opportunities to spot deer, foxes, and rare birds like the osprey.

- **Interpretive Trails**: Some of the hiking trails in the park have informative signs explaining the local flora and fauna, making it an educational experience for wildlife enthusiasts.

2. The Côte d'Or: Vineyards and Scenic Valleys
2.1. Rolling Vineyards
- **Overview:** The Côte d'Or is famous for its vineyards, but beyond the rows of grapevines, it also features scenic valleys and low hills that are home to a wide range of wildlife. Walking through the vineyards offers a chance to see small mammals like hedgehogs, hares, and a variety of birdlife.
- **Grape Harvest Season**: If you visit during the harvest season, you'll witness the vineyards buzzing with activity, and you may even spot wildlife attracted by the ripe grapes.

2.2. The Hautes-Côtes de Nuits
- **Overview:** This lesser-known area of the Côte d'Or features a more rugged landscape with limestone hills and small valleys. It's a great spot for hiking and wildlife watching, particularly for bird species such as the barn owl, red kite, and peregrine falcon.
- **Wildlife**: In addition to birds, the area is home to rabbits, foxes, and the occasional wild boar.

3. Burgundy's Rivers and Wetlands
Burgundy's rivers and wetlands are teeming with life, offering the chance to explore diverse ecosystems and spot unique species of birds and aquatic creatures.

3.1. Loire River
- **Overview**: The Loire River, which runs through parts of Burgundy, is home to a rich variety of aquatic and bird species. Along its banks, you can find herons, storks, and kingfishers, while the waters are filled with fish like trout, carp, and pike.
- **Fishing**: For those interested in angling, the Loire offers some of the best fishing spots in the region. You may catch zander, catfish, or perch.

3.2. Val de Loire Natural Reserve
- **Overview:** This wetland area is a critical habitat for migratory birds. During the winter months, species like the greylag goose, white stork, and cormorant can be seen.
- **Wildlife** Watching: Birdwatchers flock to the reserve to see these migratory birds, as well as other wildlife like the European otter and water vole.

4. Vineyards as Ecosystems: The Biodiversity of Burgundy's Terroirs

Beyond being places of wine production, Burgundy's vineyards are rich ecosystems. Many vineyards practice biodiversity-friendly farming, encouraging a balance between agriculture and wildlife.

4.1. Pollinators and Beneficial Insects

- **Bees and butterflies** are common in Burgundy's vineyards, particularly those that follow organic or biodynamic practices. These pollinators are crucial to maintaining the health of the ecosystem.
- **Other Beneficial Insects**: Ladybugs, spiders, and predatory beetles help control pests naturally, which supports sustainable farming practices in the region.

4.2. Wildlife in the Vines

- **Hares** and **rabbits** are often seen darting between rows of vines, while foxes and wild boars may roam through the vineyards in the more rural areas.
- **Birdlife**: Species such as the hoopoe, swallow, and buzzard can often be spotted in the vineyards, hunting for insects or small prey.

5. Hidden Caves and Limestone Cliffs

5.1. Caves of Arcy-sur-Cure

- **Overview:** These limestone caves are not only an important prehistoric site but also home to a number of bats, including the greater mouse-eared bat and common pipistrelle.
- **Wildlife Experience**: Guided tours of the caves will often include discussions about the unique ecosystem within, and you may have the chance to see the bats up close in their natural habitat.

5.2. Limestone Cliffs in Saône-et-Loire

Overview: These cliffs are home to birds of prey such as the peregrine falcon and the golden eagle. Rock climbers and hikers will enjoy both the challenge and the chance to spot these majestic birds in flight.

6. Conservation and Wildlife Protection in Burgundy

Burgundy is committed to preserving its natural heritage. Numerous conservation efforts are in place to protect the region's flora and fauna.

6.1. Wildlife Reserves

The Morvan Regional Natural Park and other protected areas serve as crucial habitats for many of the region's endangered species, such as the European otter and the black stork.

6.2. Sustainable Wine Practices

Many vineyards in Burgundy are moving towards organic and biodynamic farming, which promotes biodiversity and protects the local ecosystem from the harmful effects of pesticides and chemical fertilizers.

CHAPTER SEVEN

Planning Your Trip

Sample Itineraries

3-Day Itinerary: Best of Burgundy
This 3-day itinerary is designed to give you a taste of Burgundy's rich heritage, world-renowned wines, and stunning natural landscapes. Perfect for a quick getaway, this itinerary covers must-see landmarks, culinary experiences, and scenic views.

Day 1: Explore the Heart of Burgundy – Dijon and Beaune
Morning
- **Arrive in Dijon**: Start your day in Dijon, Burgundy's capital city.
  - **Palace of the Dukes and the Musée des Beaux-Arts**: Dive into Dijon's rich history at this impressive former royal residence.
  - **Les Halles Market**: Visit this lively market designed by Gustave Eiffel for a taste of Burgundy's gourmet products (cheeses, mustard, and pastries).

Lunch

- **Lunch in Dijon**: Enjoy a traditional meal at Maison Millière, a charming 15th-century restaurant.

Afternoon

- **Beaune – Wine Capital of Burgundy**: Drive or take the train to Beaune, about 40 minutes from Dijon.
- **Hôtel-Dieu (Hospices de Beaune):** Explore this stunning 15th-century charitable hospital, a landmark of Gothic architecture.
- **Wine Tasting at Local Wineries**: Visit wineries in the Côte de Beaune region. Try a wine tasting at Patriarche Père et Fils, known for its vast underground wine cellars.

Dinner

- **Dinner at Le Jardin des Remparts:** A Michelin-starred restaurant in Beaune where you can indulge in Burgundy's finest cuisine and wines.

Overnight

- **Stay in Beaune:** Spend the night in one of Beaune's boutique hotels, such as Hôtel Le Cep.

Day 2: Wine, Vineyards, and Medieval Towns
Morning

- **Wine Route:** Route des Grands Crus: Begin the day with a scenic drive or bike ride along the Route des Grands Crus, one of France's most famous wine routes.
- **Visit Vineyards in Gevrey-Chambertin**: Known for producing world-class red wines, stop at Domaine Armand Rousseau for a private tasting.

Lunch

- **Lunch at a Vineyard:** Enjoy lunch at a vineyard restaurant, such as La Table d'Olivier Leflaive in Puligny-Montrachet, where you can pair local dishes with wine straight from the vineyard.

Afternoon

- **Explore Châteauneuf-en-Auxois**: After lunch, visit this well-preserved medieval village perched on a hill with panoramic views of the surrounding countryside.
  - **Château de Châteauneuf**: Take a guided tour of the château and learn about its history.

Dinner
- **Dinner in Pommard:** Visit Le Cellier Volnaysien for a relaxed dinner, offering a farm-to-table experience with local wines.

Overnight
- **Stay in Pommard or Beaune:** Spend the night in a cozy vineyard lodge or head back to Beaune for a restful night.

Day 3: Natural Beauty and Outdoor Adventures in the Morvan
Morning
- **Day Trip to Morvan Regional Natural Park**: Drive to Morvan, about an hour from Beaune, for a day immersed in nature.
  - **Lac des Settons**: Walk around the scenic lake or rent a kayak for a peaceful morning on the water.

Lunch
- **Picnic in the Park:** Pack a picnic with Burgundy cheeses, baguettes, and wine, or enjoy lunch at a lakeside café.

Afternoon

- **Hiking and Exploring Nature:** Choose one of the many hiking trails in the park to enjoy the stunning forests, hills, and wildlife. Alternatively, visit Bibracte, an ancient Gallic archaeological site nearby.

Evening Return
- **Return to Beaune or Dijon**: End your trip back in Beaune or Dijon, with time for a farewell dinner at one of the local bistros.

7-Day Adventure: Wine, Nature, and History

For those seeking a more in-depth exploration of Burgundy, this 7-day adventure covers the region's finest wines, beautiful nature, and captivating history, ensuring you experience Burgundy's essence.

Day 1: Arrival in Dijon
- **Explore Dijon:** Begin your journey in the capital of Burgundy. Visit the Palace of the Dukes, Musée des Beaux-Arts, and stroll through the old town's charming streets.
- **Dinner at Loiseau des Ducs:** Dine at a Michelin-starred restaurant.
- **Overnight**: Stay in Dijon at Grand Hotel La Cloche.

Day 2: Dijon and the Wine Route
- **Morning:** Continue exploring Dijon with a visit to Notre-Dame of Dijon and the Musée de la Vie Bourguignonne.
- **Lunch**: Have lunch at Café Gourmand.
- **Afternoon**: Drive along the Route des Grands Crus, stopping at wineries in Gevrey-Chambertin and Nuits-Saint-Georges.
- **Overnight**: Stay in a vineyard hotel in Nuits-Saint-Georges.

Day 3: Beaune and the Hospices
- **Morning:** Travel to Beaune and tour the Hospices de Beaune.
- **Lunch**: Enjoy lunch at Le P'tit Paradis in Beaune.
- **Afternoon**: Visit Domaine de la Romanée-Conti for a tasting session.
- **Evening**: Relax with a glass of wine in Beaune's old town.
- **Overnight**: Stay at Hôtel Le Cep.

Day 4: Châteauneuf-en-Auxois and the Morvan
- **Morning:** Visit Châteauneuf-en-Auxois.
- **Lunch**: Have lunch in the village.

- **Afternoon**: Drive to Morvan Regional Natural Park. Hike the Sentier des Crêtes or enjoy the views around Lac des Settons.
- **Overnight**: Stay at a countryside retreat near Lac des Settons.

Day 5: Historical Sites and Wine Villages
- **Morning**: Visit the Abbey of Fontenay, a UNESCO World Heritage Site.
- **Lunch**: Have lunch in Semur-en-Auxois, a picturesque medieval town.
- **Afternoon**: Visit Pommard and Meursault for wine tastings.
- **Overnight**: Stay in Meursault at a boutique wine estate.

Day 6: Vézelay and Wine Tasting in Chablis
- **Morning:** Head to Vézelay, a hilltop village with a stunning basilica.
- **Lunch**: Lunch in Vézelay.
- **Afternoon**: Drive to Chablis for wine tasting at Domaine William Fèvre.
- **Overnight**: Stay at a wine estate in Chablis.

Day 7: Santenay and Farewell
- **Morning:** Visit the thermal town of Santenay and its surrounding vineyards.

- **Lunch**: Lunch at Auberge de la Côte d'Or in Santenay.
- **Afternoon**: Relax and take a final scenic drive through the Côte de Beaune.
- **Evening**: Head back to Dijon or Beaune for a final dinner.

Specialized Itineraries: Wine Enthusiasts and Family Trips

Wine Enthusiasts: Burgundy's Ultimate Wine Experience (5 Days)

This itinerary is tailored for wine lovers looking to delve deep into Burgundy's renowned vineyards and wine culture. Expect private tastings, vineyard tours, and exclusive wine-pairing meals.

Day 1: Welcome to Dijon and Côte de Nuits
Morning

- **Arrive in Dijon:** Start with a light exploration of the city, famous for its mustard and wine heritage.
  - **Visit the Musée des Beaux-Arts**: Admire the art and history before your wine adventure begins.

Lunch

- **Lunch at La Maison des Cariatides**: Savor Burgundian cuisine in this Michelin-starred restaurant.

Afternoon
- **Côte de Nuits Wine Route**: Explore Burgundy's Pinot Noir heartland. Stop in Gevrey-Chambertin and Vosne-Romanée for vineyard tours and tastings.
    - **Private Tasting at Domaine Armand Rousseau**: One of the premier estates in Gevrey-Chambertin, known for its world-class red wines.

Dinner
- **Dinner at Le Millésime** in Chambolle-Musigny, pairing local dishes with the region's finest wines.

Overnight
- **Stay in Nuits-Saint-Georges** at a vineyard estate like La Gentilhommière.

Day 2: The Legendary Vineyards of Côte de Beaune Morning

- **Hospices de Beaune**: Begin the day in Beaune with a tour of this iconic charitable hospital, followed by a visit to its wine cellars.

Lunch
- **Lunch at Le Bistro de l'Hôtel in Beaune:** Enjoy wine and food pairings.

Afternoon
- **Vineyards of Pommard and Meursault**: Spend the afternoon touring wineries in Pommard (known for full-bodied reds) and Meursault (famous for white wines).
    - **Tasting at Domaine des Comtes Lafon:** Renowned for producing some of Burgundy's finest Chardonnays.

Dinner
- **Dinner at Le Montrachet in Puligny-Montrachet**: Pair gourmet food with the region's celebrated white wines.

Overnight
- **Stay at Hôtel Le Cep in Beaune**, offering luxurious accommodations close to the vineyards.

Day 3: Chassagne-Montrachet and Wine Workshops
Morning

- **Chassagne-Montrachet Wine Tour**: Start your day at the famous Chassagne-Montrachet vineyards, known for both reds and whites.
- **Tasting at Domaine Jean-Marc Pillot:** A unique opportunity to taste their exclusive bottles.

Lunch
- **Lunch at La Table d'Olivier Leflaive:** Enjoy a meal at this family-run vineyard restaurant, paired with wines from Puligny-Montrachet.

Afternoon
- **Wine Blending Workshop:** Participate in a hands-on workshop where you learn the art of blending wines.

Dinner
- **Dinner at Ma Cuisine in Beaune,** where the wine list features an extensive collection of local vintages.

Overnight
- **Stay in Beaune at Hôtel Le Cep** or a nearby wine estate.

Day 4: Chablis and Northern Burgundy

Morning

- **Day Trip to Chablis:** Travel to northern Burgundy to explore Chablis, home to some of the world's best Chardonnay.
- **Tasting at Domaine William Fèvre:** Taste Chablis wines with distinctive minerality.

Lunch

- **Lunch at Au Fil du Zinc in Chablis,** known for its modern cuisine paired with Chablis wines.

Afternoon

- **Visit to Chablis Vineyards**: Explore the Grand Cru vineyards such as Les Clos and Les Preuses.

Dinner

- **Dinner in Chablis**: Enjoy your final evening with a wine-pairing dinner at Hostellerie des Clos.

Overnight

- **Stay at Hostellerie des Clos,** a boutique hotel surrounded by vineyards.

Day 5: Farewell to Burgundy
Morning

- **Breakfast and Final Tastings**: Enjoy a leisurely breakfast followed by a visit to a local vineyard for a final tasting before heading back.

Family-Friendly Trip: Burgundy with Kids (5 Days)

This family itinerary is designed to offer a blend of outdoor activities, cultural experiences, and family-friendly attractions, ensuring both parents and kids enjoy their time in Burgundy.

Day 1: Arrival and Exploring Dijon
Morning

- **Arrive in Dijon**: Start with a family-friendly walking tour through the city's historical center.
  - **The Owl Trail (Parcours de la Chouette):** Follow this interactive trail through Dijon, designed to be fun for kids, where they can spot owl markers around the city's landmarks.

Lunch

- **Lunch at DZ'envies:** A family-friendly restaurant offering modern Burgundian cuisine.

Afternoon

- **Visit the Jardin Darcy and Fountain**: Take a relaxing stroll in Dijon's most famous park.

166

- **Dijon Mustard Shop Visit:** Introduce the kids to the famous Maille Mustard Shop for a fun tasting experience.

Dinner
- **Dinner at a family-friendly bistro** like **Le Coin Caché**, offering regional cuisine.

Overnight
- **Stay in Dijon** at **Holiday Inn Dijon** or another family-friendly hotel with amenities for children.

Day 2: Castles and Outdoor Adventures
Morning
- **Visit Château de Châteauneuf:** Head to this medieval castle, which looks like it's straight out of a fairy tale, offering engaging tours for kids.

Lunch
- **Picnic in Châteauneuf:** Pack a picnic lunch to enjoy in the castle's scenic surroundings.

Afternoon
- **Day Trip to Morvan Regional Natural Park:** Head to the Morvan for outdoor activities such as:
  - **Lac des Settons:** Rent paddleboats or kayaks, perfect for families.

- Hiking or Biking: Choose short family-friendly trails through the park.

Dinner
- Dinner in a **lakeside café** at Lac des Settons, serving kid-friendly meals.

Overnight
- **Stay in the Morvan:** Book a family lodge in the Morvan region for an immersive nature experience.

Day 3: Family Fun in Beaune and Vineyards
Morning
- **Travel to Beaune**: Start your day with a visit to the Hôtel-Dieu. Kids will love exploring the colorful roof and the museum.

Lunch
- **Lunch at Le Conty**: A family-friendly spot in Beaune that offers simple, fresh dishes.

Afternoon
- **Bike Ride through Vineyards**: Rent bikes and enjoy a family ride through the scenic vineyards surrounding Beaune.

- Kid-Friendly Wine Tours: Some vineyards, like Domaine Drouhin, offer tours that are accessible and engaging for older children, where they can learn about winemaking.

Dinner
- Dinner at **Pizzeria des Halles** in Beaune: A casual spot with pizza and pasta options for kids.

Overnight
- Stay at a family-friendly hotel in Beaune, such as Les Jardins de Lois.

Day 4: Burgundy Adventure Day
Morning
- **Hot Air Balloon Ride**: Start your day with a family-friendly hot air balloon ride over Burgundy's vineyards and landscapes, offering spectacular views.

Lunch
- **Lunch in a Vineyard:** Book a lunch at La Table d'Olivier Leflaive, where kids can enjoy simple dishes while adults indulge in wine pairings.

Afternoon

- **Horseback Riding in the Morvan**: Book a family horseback riding tour through the scenic countryside, suitable for all ages.

Dinner
- **Dinner at a Farm Stay**: Enjoy a farm-to-table experience at a local agriturismo.

Overnight
- **Stay at a Farm Stay:** Book a family room at a farm stay, where kids can interact with animals and learn about rural life.

Day 5: Relaxing Day and Departure
Morning
- **Visit a Local Market:** Stroll through a local market in Beaune or Dijon and pick up fresh produce, cheeses, and snacks.

Lunch
- **Lunch at a Local Café:** Enjoy a relaxed meal in Beaune or Dijon.

Afternoon

- **Relax at the Pool:** Spend the afternoon at your hotel's pool or take a short walk through the surrounding vineyards.

Departure
- **Farewell to Burgundy**: Depending on your schedule, spend the rest of the day relaxing before heading home.

Useful Tips for Travelers
Packing Lists, Budgeting, and Language Barriers

Packing List for Burgundy Travelers
Essentials
- **Passport and Identification**: Ensure your passport is valid for at least six months beyond your travel dates. Keep copies of important documents like visas and travel insurance.
- **Travel Insurance**: Especially important if you're planning outdoor adventures.
- **Credit Cards and Cash**: Carry both for convenience; many smaller establishments may only accept cash.

- **Travel Adapters**: France uses Type C and Type E plugs (230V). Pack a universal adapter.
- **Mobile Charger**: For staying connected with GPS and travel apps.

Clothing

- **Layered Clothing:** Burgundy's weather can be unpredictable. Pack layers such as sweaters, light jackets, and scarves.
- **Comfortable Walking Shoes**: Essential for walking through vineyards, villages, and towns.
- **Dressy Outfit**: For dining at upscale restaurants or attending cultural events.
- **Rain Gear:** A lightweight rain jacket or umbrella, as Burgundy can experience showers year-round.

Seasonal Considerations

- **Spring/Summer**: Sunglasses, sunscreen, and hats are essential for vineyard tours and outdoor activities.
- **Fall/Winter**: Warmer clothing, gloves, and a hat for colder weather, especially if visiting during the harvest season in fall.

Wine Enthusiast Gear

- **Wine Carrier**: If you plan to purchase wine, bring a wine carrier or protective case.

- **Wine Journal**: Keep track of the different wines you try throughout the region.

Miscellaneous
- **Reusable Water Bottle**: Stay hydrated during hikes and vineyard visits.
- **Daypack or Tote:** A small bag for day trips to carry snacks, water, and essentials.
- **Portable Phone Charger**: Handy for long days of exploring.

Budgeting Tips for Traveling to Burgundy

Accommodation
- **Luxury Hotels**: Expect to spend €150–€500 per night for high-end hotels like Hôtel Le Cep or Château de Gilly.
- **Mid-Range**: For comfortable accommodations, budget around €80–€150 per night in places like boutique hotels or farm stays.
- **Budget Options**: Hostels and guesthouses can range from €40–€80 per night. Airbnb is also a

good option for affordable stays, especially in smaller villages.

Food and Dining

- **Luxury Dining**: Michelin-starred restaurants in Burgundy will cost €100–€200 per person.
- **Mid-Range**: Bistros and family-run restaurants offer meals for around €20–€50 per person.
- **Budget Eats**: Local bakeries, markets, and casual dining spots can provide meals for €10–€15.

Transportation

- **Car Rentals**: Renting a car in Burgundy typically costs between €30–€70 per day, plus fuel. Look for deals when booking in advance.
- **Trains and Buses**: Public transportation between cities (e.g., Dijon to Beaune) costs around €10–€20 per ticket. A regional rail pass can help save money on longer trips.
- **Bicycle Rentals**: Renting a bike to tour vineyards costs around €15–€25 per day.

Wine Tasting and Tours

- **Private Wine Tastings**: Premium experiences can range from €50–€150 per person, depending on the estate.
- **Group Tours**: Wine tours generally cost €30–€80 per person.

- **Free Tastings**: Some wineries offer complimentary tastings if you make a purchase.

Sightseeing and Activities
- **Museum and Monument Fees**: Entry fees for sites like the Hospices de Beaune or Abbey of Fontenay range from €5–€15.
- **Outdoor Activities**: Hiking in the Morvan is generally free, while activities like hot air ballooning can cost €200 or more.

Language Barriers: What to Expect and How to Overcome Them

While Burgundy is a tourist-friendly region, English may not always be widely spoken, particularly in smaller towns and villages. Here's how to navigate the language barriers:

Common French Phrases for Travelers
- Bonjour (Hello) / Bonsoir (Good evening)
- Merci (Thank you)
- S'il vous plaît (Please)
- Parlez-vous anglais? (Do you speak English?)

- Où est…? (Where is…?)
- L'addition, s'il vous plaît (The bill, please)

Helpful Tools
- **Language Apps**: Use apps like Google Translate or Duolingo to learn basic phrases and communicate effectively.
- **Phrasebook**: Carry a small French phrasebook or download an app for offline use.
- **Politeness Counts**: Even a few French words and politeness go a long way. Locals appreciate the effort, and you're more likely to receive assistance.

Tips for Communicating
- **Slow Down:** Speak slowly and clearly if someone is struggling with English.
- **Use Gestures**: Don't be afraid to use hand gestures or pointing to help explain yourself.
- **Hotel Concierge**: Many higher-end hotels have English-speaking staff who can help with bookings, directions, and translations.

Eco-Friendly Travel Tips for Burgundy
Burgundy's stunning landscapes and commitment to sustainable wine production make it an ideal destination

for eco-conscious travelers. Here are ways to minimize your environmental footprint while enjoying the region.

Transportation
- **Use Public Transport**: Trains and buses are efficient and eco-friendly ways to travel between major towns and villages like Dijon, Beaune, and Chalon-sur-Saône.
- **Bike Tours:** Opt for cycling tours along the Route des Grands Crus or in the Morvan instead of driving. Many towns offer bike rentals, and dedicated cycling paths make this an enjoyable experience.
- **Carpooling and Electric Cars**: If you need to rent a car, consider hybrid or electric vehicles. Look for charging stations in larger towns.

Sustainable Accommodation
- **Eco-Friendly Hotels:** Choose accommodations that prioritize sustainability. Look for Green Key or EcoLabel certified hotels, such as Hôtel de la Cloche in Dijon.
- **Farm Stays:** Opt for agritourism or eco-lodges where you can stay on organic farms and enjoy farm-to-table dining.

Responsible Wine Tourism
- **Organic and Biodynamic Wineries:** Visit eco-friendly wineries like Domaine de la

Vougeraie, known for its biodynamic practices. Many Burgundy vineyards are adopting sustainable farming methods, making your wine tasting experiences more eco-friendly.

- **Wine Purchase with Minimal Packaging**: If you buy wine, bring a reusable wine carrier or purchase from producers who use minimal packaging or offer bottle reuse programs.

Reduce Plastic Waste

- **Reusable Water Bottles:** Burgundy has clean and safe tap water, so carry a reusable water bottle to reduce plastic waste.
- **Bring Your Own Shopping Bag**: Many local markets encourage the use of reusable shopping bags, so pack your own for trips to food markets or wineries.

Support Local and Sustainable Dining

- **Farm-to-Table Restaurants:** Choose restaurants that source their ingredients locally and practice sustainability. Restaurants like L'Arôme in Beaune focus on organic and local produce.
- **Seasonal and Organic Choices:** Opt for meals made with seasonal and organic ingredients. Burgundy's markets are filled with fresh, local produce.

Respect Nature and Wildlife

- **Stay on Trails:** When hiking or cycling in the Morvan Regional Natural Park, stick to marked trails to preserve the ecosystem and avoid disturbing wildlife.
- **Leave No Trace:** Carry any trash with you when exploring natural areas, and avoid picking flowers or disturbing local flora and fauna.

Essential Apps and Digital Tools for Tourists Visiting Burgundy

To make your Burgundy adventure smooth and hassle-free, the right digital tools can be a huge help. Here are some essential apps and digital tools that will enhance your travel experience by helping you with navigation, language, booking, and staying connected.

1. Navigation and Maps

Google Maps

- **Best For:** General navigation, public transport routes, and walking directions.
- **Features**: Offers offline maps (download Burgundy maps before your trip), restaurant and

hotel reviews, and detailed directions to tourist sites.
- **Tip:** Pin your key locations like hotels, restaurants, and tourist spots for easy access.

MAPS.ME
- **Best For:** Offline navigation.
- **Features**: Download the Burgundy region map and access it even without data. Perfect for hiking and cycling trails in remote areas like the Morvan Regional Natural Park.

2. Language and Translation
Google Translate
- **Best For:** Translating French to English and vice versa.
- **Features**: Offers offline mode when you download French language packs, voice-to-text translation, and camera translation (point at menus, signs, etc.).
- **Tip**: Use the conversation mode for real-time translations when talking to locals.

Duolingo
- **Best For:** Learning basic French before and during your trip.

- **Features**: Fun, interactive lessons that help you pick up essential phrases in French, even if you're a beginner.
- **Tip**: Try a few lessons on greetings, directions, and dining before your trip for smoother interactions.

3. Currency Conversion and Budgeting

XE Currency Converter
- **Best For:** Real-time currency conversions.
- **Features**: Keep track of the latest exchange rates for EUR (Euros) to your home currency. It works offline, saving the last updated rates.
- **Tip**: Use this app when shopping, dining, or booking tours to quickly check the cost in your own currency.

Trail Wallet
- **Best For**: Travel budgeting.
- **Features**: Helps you track daily expenses, categorize spending, and stick to your budget during your trip. You can input your own currency and set daily or overall trip budgets.
- **Tip**: Input your accommodation, food, transport, and activity costs to keep your finances in check while enjoying Burgundy.

4. Transportation

SNCF Connect
- **Best For:** Booking train tickets across Burgundy and the rest of France.
- **Features**: Plan train trips between Dijon, Beaune, and other cities. The app provides real-time schedules, platform information, and e-tickets.
- **Tip**: Book tickets in advance for the best prices and ensure you download them for offline access.

Blablacar
- **Best For:** Carpooling.
- **Features**: Share rides with locals for affordable travel between towns. It's often cheaper than trains or buses, and you get to meet people on the way.
- **Tip**: Check reviews and ratings of drivers before booking for a safer ride.

Dijon Mobilités
- **Best For:** Navigating public transport in Dijon.
- **Features**: Real-time schedules for buses and trams in Dijon, including routes and fare

information. You can buy tickets via the app as well.

- **Tip**: Use this app to get around Dijon's city center easily without a car.

Booking.com

- **Best For:** Booking hotels, B&Bs, and farm stays.
- **Features**: Offers a wide variety of accommodations across Burgundy, from luxury hotels to budget-friendly options. You can filter by user ratings, price, and amenities.
- **Tip**: Book accommodations with free cancellation in case your travel plans change.

Airbnb

- **Best For:** Staying in unique, local homes or boutique guesthouses.
- **Features**: Choose from affordable farm stays, cottages, or homes in Burgundy's villages for a more local experience.
- **Tip**: Look for Airbnb options in wine regions like Chablis or Beaune for an immersive stay close to vineyards.

La Fourchette (The Fork)

- **Best For**: Restaurant reservations.

- **Features**: Book tables at Burgundy's best restaurants, read reviews, and even receive discounts at some spots.
- **Tip**: Use this app to reserve tables at popular restaurants, especially during peak tourist seasons or festivals.

6. Wine and Food Apps

Vivino

- **Best For:** Wine recommendations and reviews.
- **Features**: Scan wine labels at local vineyards or stores to get ratings, reviews, and food pairing tips. You can also keep track of wines you like during your Burgundy tasting tours.
- **Tip**: Use Vivino when purchasing wine directly from vineyards to ensure you get the best bottles.

Yelp

- **Best For:** Finding restaurants and cafes.
- **Features**: Browse user reviews for eateries, bars, and cafes across Burgundy. Filter by price, cuisine type, or user ratings.
- **Tip:** Use Yelp to discover hidden gem restaurants or cafes that aren't always listed in travel guides.

7. Weather and Safety

Météo France

- **Best For:** Accurate local weather forecasts.

- **Features**: Real-time updates for Burgundy's weather, including hourly forecasts and weather alerts. Essential if you're planning outdoor activities like hiking or vineyard tours.
- **Tip**: Check the forecast each morning to decide whether you need rain gear, sunscreen, or warm layers for the day.

Sitata

- **Best For**: Travel safety updates.
- **Features**: Provides real-time travel safety alerts, health advisories, and tips for staying safe in unfamiliar places. It also offers access to nearby hospitals and pharmacies.
- **Tip**: Set Burgundy as your travel destination to receive localized safety updates.

8. Eco-Friendly and Sustainable Travel

HappyCow

- **Best For:** Finding vegetarian and vegan restaurants.
- **Features**: Search for eco-conscious, plant-based dining options in towns like Dijon, Beaune, and beyond.
- **Tip**: Use this app to locate restaurants that offer local and sustainable food, supporting Burgundy's farm-to-table movement.

Too Good To Go

- **Best For**: Reducing food waste.
- **Features**: Get discounted meals from restaurants, cafes, and bakeries by purchasing food that would otherwise go to waste. Great for budget-conscious and eco-friendly travelers.
- **Tip**: Check for last-minute deals at local bakeries or restaurants during your stay.

Conclusion: Embrace the Burgundy Experience

As you prepare for your adventure in Burgundy, this guide aims to be your trusted companion, helping you navigate the rich tapestry of history, culture, and natural beauty that this enchanting region has to offer. From the rolling vineyards and quaint villages to the bustling cities steeped in heritage, Burgundy is a destination that invites exploration and discovery.

Whether you're indulging in the world-renowned wines, savoring the local cuisine, or embarking on outdoor adventures, Burgundy promises a unique blend of experiences that cater to every traveler's taste. The warmth of the locals, the vibrant festivals, and the picturesque landscapes create an atmosphere that resonates long after your visit.

Remember to immerse yourself in the local customs and traditions, allowing yourself to connect with the heart of Burgundy. Be open to new experiences, from trying local delicacies to engaging with artisans and winemakers, as these interactions will enrich your journey.

With the knowledge and resources provided in this guide, you're well-equipped to embark on an unforgettable journey through Burgundy in 2025. Embrace the adventure, savor every moment, and take home cherished memories that will last a lifetime.

Printed in Dunstable, United Kingdom

69242214R00107